The Family that Couldn't Sleep at Night

and Other True Stories of Murder and Mayhem

Bruce Rubenstein

**CALUMET
EDITIONS**
Minneapolis

**CALUMET
EDITIONS**
Minneapolis

SECOND EDITION DECEMBER 2022

10 9 8 7 6 5 4 3 2
ISBN: 978-1-960250-57-5

Book and cover design by Gary Lindberg

Other Books by Bruce Rubenstein

Smoke
The Key Man
Greed, Rage, and Love Gone Wrong
The Rockwell Heist

The Family That Couldn't Sleep at Night

and Other True Stories of Murder and Mayhem

Bruce Rubenstein

The Stories

Foreword

These stories were originally published between 1983 and 2004, but I've remained interested in all of them, and they have been revised and updated as new information became available. For purposes of clarity the tense in which they were originally written has been retained, so when someone "says" something he or she probably "said" it a long time ago. But in some cases they just said it recently.

The title story, the oldest, is a case in point. After it appeared, many people who knew various members of The Family That Couldn't Sleep at Night, and had been silent for years about the pathologies of that strange household, went to great lengths to contact me and provide their insights. Things I found out as recently as 2005 (from the son of the youngest child, who was five years old when the events I describe in this book happened) are incorporated into the version that appears here.

The Family That Couldn't Sleep at Night

The Family That Couldn't Sleep at Night

This story appeared in *Sweet Potato*, a Minneapolis weekly, in 1981. The editor said he needed a rationale for publishing something about an event that happened in the 1950s, and he came up with a good one. He wrote an editor's note about how the murder of a Minneapolis policeman earlier that year was becoming an issue in the Mayor's race—"But it was not the most famous cop killing in the annals of the Minneapolis Police Department. In 1957, three brothers named O'Kasick shot two Minneapolis policemen, one fatally. That slaying and the subsequent hunt for the notorious O'Kasicks occupied media attention like few killings in the city's history."

The igneous rock underlying the St. Cloud, Minnesota region consists almost entirely of high-quality granite, both pink and gray, that can be quarried, slabbed and sold for a variety of purposes. Granite still makes a stately staircase, or a handsome gravestone and before the era of reinforced concrete it was the material of choice for prison construction. Granite is not especially serviceable as a grinding agent, but in a pinch it will do. Witness the innumerable weapons that have been fashioned by rubbing pieces of metal against the gray walls of the St. Cloud state prison. In fact, the same qualities that make St. Cloud Gray so highly favored for mausoleums and prisons—density, impenetrability, mass, make it useful for sharpening blades.

There are problems, though, practical matters that must be recognized and addressed. Guards are always looking for scratches on the grinding surface. If cell walls were made of something harder, diamonds maybe, there wouldn't be any scratches to hide, a possibility that prisoners daydream about. But if daydreams came true prisons would be empty, so the inmates make do with what they have, then cover the marred surface with a carefully placed footlocker, a picture of mom, any old thing.

There is no record of what inmate No. 22121 used to hide the scratches on his cell wall during the first half of September 1958. The 22,120 inmates who preceded him had developed a body of knowledge about making knives, so it couldn't have been much of a problem. All we know for sure is that sometime in early September, while the junior guards walked the dog shift, and the solid fifty percent of any prison's population who are plagued by insomnia turned things over in their minds, No. 22121 took to rubbing a table knife with a round end against the wall of his cell.

Approximately ten hours of work are required to produce a proper point, and sleep eventually overwhelms even the most troubled mind, so his task must have consumed the better part of two weeks. He probably lay on his side, face to the wall, footlocker pulled slightly askew, and scraped. He used a downward stroke because an up-down motion will produce vibrations, even through granite, and those vibrations might reach the ear of a guard. So it was down down down on one side, then down down down on the other.

By the second week the point was no longer blunt to the touch. Now the blade had to be ground at an angle, requiring either a circular or back and forth motion. Two or three passes and a pause. Two or three more. No vibrations.

By September 15, No. 22121 had managed to fashion a deadly weapon out of a standard institutional table knife. He told the guard on duty that morning that he was feeling sick, and didn't want to go to his job in the tailor shop. The guard said okay, checked to make sure the cell was locked, and continued on his rounds. The moment he left, No. 22121 pulled his blanket over his head, plunged the knife into his stomach, drew it out, and stabbed himself again.

Neither wound was immediately fatal. At that point it may have crossed his mind to stick the knife in his heart, but he would have resisted the impulse, remembering the time a year ago almost to the day when he hid in a thicket near the bodies of his dead brothers and turned his pistol on himself. The bullet had nicked his heart, leaving him alive but permanently weakened.

So 20-year-old James O'Kasick, the last survivor of the infamous O'Kasick gang, pushed the crudely fashioned knife into his stomach for the third time, curled up around the hilt, and slipped into unconsciousness. He died half an hour later in an ambulance speeding toward St. Cloud Hospital, while attendants, for reasons that wouldn't have made any sense to him, tried to save his life.

Dad

Everett Warren Allen was walking down Franklin Avenue one winter night when the snow came whipping in on a bitter west wind, and the dog shit on the sidewalk was frozen hard enough to stub your toe. He didn't have anything but a pint of wine, four dollars, a wrist watch, and a pocket knife to scare the muggers away. He stopped at the corner, snuck a hit of wine, then capped the bottle again with his numb fingers, all the while peeking down the side street to see if anyone was watching. Somebody was. Hold on there, partner, he heard the guy say.

Maybe the arc light swinging in the wind cast a feral glint off Michael O'Kasick's lazy eye. It certainly shed enough light for Everett to recognize one of the meanest drunks on the Avenue heading his way.

That you Mike? Everett said, as Mike drew near.

Mike didn't answer. He just stood there, glaring. A gust of wind stung the back of Everett's bare neck. He pushed his hands into his pockets and felt for his knife. There it was, under the Zippo. He knew right then he didn't have the guts to use it.

Wouldn't have a few bucks to spare? Mike asked. Naw, I ain't got nothing, Everett replied. Yeah, you do, you've got that watch, Mike said. I seen that before you put your hands in your pockets.

Can't give you that, Mike.

You son of a bitch, Mike said. Let's just see what you've got. He grabbed Everett Warren Allen by the arm, pulled him down the side street, and tried to trip him.

Everett was a lot bigger than Mike (everybody was bigger than Mike), so he didn't fall. He kept his balance and started to walk away.

Mike grabbed him again. Just a damn minute, he said, and he pulled a toy gun out of his pocket.

Now what is this crazy bastard up to? Everett thought. Am I supposed to pretend he's fooling me with that thing?

See what this is? This here is a gun!

Yeah, yeah, Everett said, and he started to walk away again.

Mike ran up and punched him on the back of his head. Everett stumbled, and Mike leaped on him and pulled him to the ground. This is a gun, you son of a bitch, HEAR ME? A GUN! He kicked Everett in the ribs.

Everett gave Mike everything he had so he wouldn't get beat up any more, even gave him what was left of the wine. Mike stuffed the bills, the knife, the watch, and the toy gun into his pockets, kicked Everett one more time just for the hell of it, then walked off up the Avenue. He paused and took a long swig from the bottle. He drained it and laughed.

YOU BASTARD, Everett heard himself yelling after Mike, and he lowered his voice abruptly. I'll get you for this, he muttered. Mike just shot him a dirty look and flung the empty bottle back in his direction. It skidded past on the snow.

An hour later Mike was bellied up to the bar at the Brite Spot, one foot on the rail and Everett's last buck tucked under an empty glass in front of him. He had a nice glow on, and he was trying to get the bartender's attention, when all of a sudden the joint hushed up, literally went silent, behind him. He turned around. There was Everett Warren Allen in the doorway with a cop.

That's him, officer, Mike O'Kasick! He done it. Watch out! He's got a gun!

Now wait a minute, Mike started to say, but the cop drew his pistol, and yelled FREEZE!

Mike froze.

Michael O'Kasick sentenced to two to fifteen years in Stillwater prison for robbery from one Everett Warren Allen, cash and items of value in the amount of $11.52: cash, $4.44; ballpoint pen, 98 cents; pocketknife, $1; watch, $5.

The Family

A probation officer who was checking on Mike once described Mrs. Florence O'Kasick as "passive, run down, beaten." A friend of the family told a St. Paul Dispatch reporter, "The old man would get drunk and beat her and the kids up. She developed a nervous disorder, and just fell apart and died one day, back in '52."

"None of us can forget mother," Doris O'Kasick told a reporter, after her brothers were killed. "She just couldn't keep up with it. She died of a broken heart."

Roger O'Kasick was the smartest one in the family, a bookworm who shut himself up in his rented room and read books from the library. He was a rebel and a scofflaw, but he never had an overdue library book. It was a matter of pride with him. When he wasn't reading, he hung around bars and pool halls, and showed off by carrying a gun. His sister Joyce called him the bitter one, the quiet one who would pick a fight for no reason at all. The family's poverty just gnawed at him, she said.

According to a social worker at Phillips Junior High, Roger had sadistic tendencies. He was sent to Red Wing

Reformatory for burglarizing a safe at Phillips when he was seventeen, and joined the army to get an early release.

For a few weeks after he was discharged, he treated his sister Doris like a girlfriend. He took her out to movies, bought her flowers, held her hand when they walked down Franklin Avenue. Doris told a reporter that she thought it was curious the way he acted.

The oldest brother, Richard, later told police that Mike O'Kasick routinely sexually assaulted his own daughters, and ignored his sons' advances toward their sisters unless he had designs on the same girl. Then he'd beat them and call them sinners.

As a child Roger was shy and ashamed of his threadbare clothes, but by 1957, when he was 26, the police described him as a flashy barroom tough who dressed in straw "boater" hats, single-breasted black sport coats, and cream-colored, draped pants that cut his patent leather shoes just so, about an inch above the heel. They said he bolstered his courage with liquor, and was prone to sudden, destructive rages.

Roger's little brother Ronnie was driving around in a stolen car one night in November 1952, with a buddy of his from Franklin Avenue. Sleet that sometimes turned to snow was falling. Mom was dead.

Ronnie wanted to get some money so he could go to California and get warm. The fuel company had cut them off, and there was no heat in the house. He'd been cold for days.

They drove slowly past the Maddox Grocery on 26th Avenue SE. This is called casing the joint, Ronnie told his pal.

It looked like an easy heist, a breeze, even with a toy gun, which was all they had. Ronnie went in while his friend waited in the car. He pointed the gun at the store owner. This is a stickup, mister, he said. Hand over all your money!

The grocer came over the counter, grabbed him by the shirt, and threw him through the storefront window. He and his buddy escaped in the stolen car, ditched it a few blocks away, and started walking back to the Avenue. The sidewalks were ankle deep in icy slush. Ronnie's hand was badly cut, and they made a few lame jokes about the trail of blood they were leaving.

Later that night Ronnie was arrested. He pleaded guilty to attempted robbery and was sentenced to the St. Cloud prison. He was 18. He got out after a year, and married a few weeks later. By the time he was 21 he had two children. He often told his wife about his early home life, how his mother had died when he and his 12 brothers and sisters were kids. He said they didn't have any money and were hungry many times. They lived in a tiny house right across the street from Phillips Junior High, so their pitiful life was on permanent display for their classmates. Sometimes the old man would get drunk on the Avenue, stagger home, but fail to make it through the door. Instead he'd pass out and spend the night in the front yard. Kids on the way to school would tease him with sticks until he came around, then run away laughing.

People seemed to agree that Ronnie was a likable guy. He had many friends around Minneapolis, good friends, according to a pal of his, who talked to a reporter in September 1957. The interview took place in a graveyard shaded by poplar trees. His friends had gotten some money together to give Ronnie a little funeral, and the press showed up, as they inevitably did at any venue that might produce some tidbit about the O'Kasick gang.

Ronnie's buddies got drunk and extolled the virtues of their deceased friend. Gusts of wind showered golden leaves down on the casket. The grave diggers stood around eyeing the mourners and the reporters, wishing it would end, wishing they could fill the hole and go get drunk themselves. It was their first celebrity funeral.

Even the *Minneapolis Star* had something good to say about Ronnie after he was buried. It said that of the three brothers, Ronnie had the least to answer for. "He shot no one, and may have been an unwilling accomplice." It was probably true. He was a mope and a sad sack, not a killer. His wife had divorced him by the time he started using a real gun to rob stores, and he spent most of his loot in a vain attempt to win her back. She called him a little guy who always wanted to be big. He was five feet three and weighed 127 pounds. He talked about buying elevator shoes, but never got around to it.

Jimmy was the youngest of the three, a brawler, more like Roger, whom he idolized, than Ronnie, whom he protected. Jimmy liked to throw hands. He approached a fistfight with such gleeful abandon that bigger kids feared him. He once knocked his father down for beating his sister Joyce. He was engaged briefly in 1954, but the girl broke it off when Jimmy beat her up.

Jimmy made his debut in the annals of the criminal justice system in June 1938. He was the "squalling infant" in the arms of his mother, a "distraught, disheveled woman, with missing teeth and a downcast demeanor," according to a report filed by a probation officer who had come by to see her husband. Little Jimmy's face and arms were blotched with angry red welts. He squirmed and yowled so vigorously that the officer inquired about his distress.

"We don't have much in the way of screens, and the mosquitoes bite us," Mrs. O'Kasick explained. "We can't sleep at night."

Dress Rehearsal

Jimmy told a social worker at Phillips that he dreamed of quitting school when he was sixteen, and he didn't go one day longer. Neither did Roger or Ronnie. They hung around 4th and Franklin until all hours of the night. They bought beer at the back door of the Shamrock Bar until they were old enough to walk in the front door. They hung out on the roof of the Tremont Apartments on 18th and Park, where they drank bottles of beer laced with vodka and threw the empties down at passing cars. Here comes another dead soldier! they yelled. Their records show numerous arrests "for investigation."

By 1956 Jimmy was in the Marines. His dad was on parole from Stillwater, working as a bellboy in the Hotel Duluth. Roger had rented a room of his own in south Minneapolis. The oldest brother, Richard, had become head of the household. Richard found Jesus at the Paul Rader chapel on Lake Street that spring, and The Lord told him to hold down two jobs so he could keep the family together. They lived in a small house on 38th Avenue S.

"Either six or seven of them lived there," according to Geraldine Donnelley, who lived across the street at the time. "We always called their place 'the renter's house' because everybody else on the block owned their homes. Other than that they didn't stand out in any way. The girls were kind of shy as I recall. You never saw much of the men."

The house had two tiny bedrooms, a scale-model living room, and a second-floor bathroom the size of a broom closet. Richard and Ronnie slept in the parlor so they wouldn't disturb the girls when they came home. Both of them stayed out late because of the nature of their work. Richard had a job as a cook at an all-night diner. Ronnie was painting houses with Roger during the day and sticking up drugstores with him at night.

Unlike Ronnie, Roger had a gift for casing the joint. Investigators who pieced together the O'Kasicks' career after the first shoot-out realized that their robberies had been planned meticulously. The robbers wore odd but effective disguises, and never asked where the money was. They knew. According to the victims, the leader was polite but insistent, assuring them that no one would get hurt unless they did something foolish, in which case they'd be shot in the head. He was the only one who spoke. He kept the discourse to a minimum and used a high, unnatural voice that the victims agreed was false.

Ashley Morse, the pharmacist at Zipp's Drug Store on 35th Avenue S., was preparing to close on a Sunday night in July 1956, when two masked men entered the store. They were "sporting rubber skull masks atop natty blue suits," according to the Minneapolis Star. They held the three customers at bay with, "a pair of matching .38s."

Morse's wife and his two teenage daughters arrived to take him home while the robbery was in progress. "Hands up," the leader squeaked. They joined the customers, and stood with their hands in the air while Morse emptied all four cash registers. He didn't volunteer to open the safe in the back room, but the leader gestured in that direction with his gun and told him to make it snappy. The robbers left with $1,800 cash.

That night police chased a vehicle answering the description of the car used in the holdup but lost it.

A few weeks later, on a warm August evening, Roger Lillemoe was watching TV in his living room. He happened to glance out the open window and saw two men wearing gas masks and carrying canvas bags enter Harold's Pharmacy on 41st and Cedar. Lillemoe didn't have a phone, so he ran to a nearby fire station. He tried to get the firemen to interrupt the robbery, but they declined and called the police instead.

Meanwhile, two pistol-toting young men were holding a clerk and the pharmacist at gunpoint. The leader issued a muffled command through his gas mask, and the pharmacist emptied the cash register into one canvas bag, and the safe into another. One of the bandits appeared nervous and anxious. As they exited through the back door, he dropped a bag full of cash containing $274 in the alley, but still managed to get away with approximately $1,000. By the time the police arrived, they had sped off in a blue car.

Gunmen with the same MO - masks, car stashed in the alley, previous knowledge of where the money was kept - robbed a pharmacy on 33rd and Nicollet a few weeks later. An alarm was sounded, and the police arrived just as the gunmen were pulling away. They headed south on Nicollet with the police in hot pursuit. Shots were exchanged. The squad car overheated so badly the engine seized. It was towed into the police garage, where the repair man discovered two bullet holes through the radiator.

Jimmy O'Kasick must have received a letter from Roger describing this incident. He was stationed in Japan when it took place, but he was able to describe it in detail during his long, rambling, semi-comatose confession in General Hospital a year later. He pinpointed it as the incident that prompted his brothers to buy three thick metal plates in a junkyard on Washington Avenue. They would be used to stop bullets in case of another shootout, something Roger fully expected, and apparently looked forward to with relish.

Jimmy was discharged from the Marines in April 1957. According to the Minneapolis Tribune, on June 28, 1957, "Three stocky gunmen wearing grotesque rubber monkey masks held up a north Minneapolis drug store, and escaped with about $1,200 after holding nine persons at bay in the store. One of them had a .45, the other two had .38s. They were all wearing dark suits and carrying cloth bags. Marlene Fennig, 17, thought she recognized one of the gunmen as a fellow employee playing a joke. She said 'Take off the mask, Leroy.' The bandit poked her with his gun and she buttoned her lip.

The leader made Arthur Knight, the store owner, go in back and open his safe. After taking the money, they fled in a blue Oldsmobile. Knight told police the bandits appeared young and nervous.

The Minneapolis police knew that a gang of stickup men were robbing pharmacies during the summers of 1956 and 1957. The robberies usually occurred around closing time. There were at least seven holdups with the same MO - masks, pistols, locations where a large sum of cash was available and precise knowledge of where it could be found. At first there were two gunmen, but the robbery of Knight's Pharmacy on the north side, and then of the Pennhurst Pharmacy on 51st and Penn Avenue S. in July 1957, involved three men.

No one ever saw their faces, but the victims noticed they were of the same smallish stature. At Knight's Pharmacy they appeared to be stocky, but the police decided that was the result of padding.

The gunmen planned their crimes carefully. On several robberies they used cars that had been stolen that day, with license plates that had been taken off other vehicles months before. They had been chased on two occasions by the police, and had shot at and disabled a squad car during one of those chases.

Despite the meticulous planning that could be inferred from their method of operation, they were nervous and anxious during the robberies.

Duel at Apache Wells

During the 1956 Christmas season, Ronnie charged $400 worth of merchandise at department stores, sold it in the bars for about $200, and used the cash to buy presents. When the bills came, it was the last straw as far as his wife was concerned. She took the kids and split.

Ronnie bought himself a blue Oldsmobile for three times what it was worth, just to ease the pain in his heart. A few months later Jimmy was discharged from the Marines. He bought a 1941 Cadillac with his mustering-out pay. So Ronnie and Jimmy had a couple cool cars to drive around in, and that's what they did most evenings that summer of 1957. They drove down Lake Street, one arm out the window and a pack of cigarettes rolled up in the sleeves of their T-shirts. They tuned their radios to the same station and played them so loud—songs like Be-Bop-A-Lula, You Ain't Nothin' But a Hound Dog, Party Doll—that adults standing at the stoplights plugged their ears. When the light changed they revved up and laid rubber. They tried drag racing down Lake Street too, but neither car had any guts. Ronnie's transmission slipped, and Jimmy's Caddy V-8 hit on about five cylinders.

Most nights they drove over to the Chat 'N Nibble on 28th Street to hustle the carhops. "You had to hold your nose when they drove in, because the exhaust that came out of that one car stunk so bad," a carhop remembered later, "but the guys were cute and they always had a few bucks to spend."

One night Ronnie and Jimmy took two carhops to the Hilltop Drive-In Theater to see a western, Duel at Apache Wells. They made out a little, sipped vodka from a bottle, and watched while the townsfolk slowly got fed up with the way the outlaws lorded it over the decent people.

Law-abiding citizens were subjected to outrageous indignities whenever the bandits came to town. They'd ride down the main drag, whooping, hollering, and shooting their six-guns in the air. They'd get into brawls at the saloon, then gallop off before the sheriff could put a posse together.

About halfway through the film they held up the stage, and when they got away with that, they thought they could get away with anything. Cattle began disappearing from nearby ranches. Half-starved calves wandered the range, bawling for their mamas. Those desperados just rode into town like they owned it. They drank rotgut by the quart and refused to pay the bar bill, cheated at cards and dared anybody to say a word, made a pass at the schoolmarm then beat the crap out of her fiancé when he came to her defense.

Jimmy went to the refreshment stand for popcorn and orange drinks, while the girls straightened their hair, smoothed their blouses and put on more lipstick. When Jimmy got back, Ronnie spiked the drinks with vodka, and they passed the popcorn around.

One of the girls dropped her barrette, and they searched for it in the dim glow of the interior light, among the lipstick-stained popcorn kernels. Jimmy found it behind an iron plate leaning against the front seat. What's that thing for anyway? his date asked. Nothing, he said. Ronnie turned out the light, and they watched the movie again.

Emboldened by the inability of upstanding people to cope with their viciousness, the robbers shot the old prospector down like a dog and stole all his gold dust. Then they descended on the Travis ranch, and treed that once-proud spread. They burned the bunkhouse, stampeded the horses and rustled the cattle. They spat in old man Travis's face, punched him in the stomach so hard he puked and laughed at his wife as she stood in the ranch house door with tears of disbelief in her eyes. How could they be so low-down? How long could the reign of terror last?

In fact, it was just about over. The sheriff and some men he deputized for the occasion caught up with the outlaws at Apache Wells. There was a shootout, in which a few good guys and a number of bad guys bit the dust. True to their code, the surviving bandits vowed they'd never be taken alive. Then I'm comin t'git'cha, said the sheriff, and by god he did. It wasn't pretty.

After the movie they stopped at the Sunset Drive-In on Central Avenue for french fries and cherry cokes. The girls got a bang out of having carhops wait on *them* for a change. It was a busman's holiday.

An ex-convict who met Ronnie in the St. Cloud prison gave the following account to the Minneapolis Star:

"I told Ronnie I'd meet up with him when I got out. It was the spring of '57. We went into business together, painting houses. He had a beat-up Oldsmobile that wasn't worth $200, but he owed 450 bucks on it. They used to take it to drive-ins, and I guess they used it for their getaway. I'd see those iron plates in it, but when I asked Ronnie what they were for he said 'nothing.' I never saw much of Roger. Nobody really knew Roger. I know he hated cops, just despised them. Ronnie and Jimmy drank two bottles of vodka the day before the shooting. They seemed in a big hurry to go someplace. That's the last I saw of them. They disappeared."

On the afternoon of Friday, August 16, 1957, Ronnie and Jimmy met up with their brother Roger. The three of them stole a green Chrysler from a parking lot on 10th and LaSalle, and drove to a wooded lot near a cemetery on 42nd Street and 4th Avenue S. They put the steel plates in place, and loaded a bag with friction tape, water, purifying tablets, surgical bandages and roofing nails to spread behind them in case of a chase.

Roger kept the guns between holdups, and he was in charge of buying bullets. While he was off fetching the arsenal, Ronnie fastened a pair of license plates they had stolen several months before over the Chrysler's plates. They hid the car in the woods behind the cemetery, ready for the robbery they'd planned for the next day.

They thought the police were no longer looking for the stolen plates, but they were wrong. The numbers were on a list taped to the dashboard of every patrol car in town.

Early Saturday evening, August 17, the O'Kasicks picked up the Chrysler and set out to rob the Red Owl Super Market on Hennepin and 24th. Ronnie and Jimmy were pretty hung over, and all three of them were more nervous than usual before a holdup, because there was more at stake. The Red Owl promised to be a big score, maybe $10,000, according to Roger.

It was a warm evening with plenty of shoppers, and lots of traffic. Ronnie was at the wheel. Roger sat next to him with a loaded pistol on his lap, and bandoliers of ammunition criss-crossed under his suit coat. Jimmy was in back with a 30-30 rifle, a metal plate propped up on the seat behind him. They all wore white ties, black shirts and straw hats.

They cruised slowly west on Lake Street, biding their time until dark, which was still twenty minutes away. It was a measure of their anxiety that they were on the street so early and so well armed, and it may have been a measure of something else. Roger called the shots, and according to many who knew him, he had an irrational hatred of policemen. He was spoiling for a fight. His behavior during the two violent episodes that would soon follow stamped him as a person with an utter disdain for death. It seemed as if he might welcome death, as long as he could take a cop or two with him.

Officers Robert Fossum and Ward Canfield were in a squad car driving west on Lake when they spotted the Chrysler a few cars ahead. Within moments they had identified the stolen plates. The Chrysler was hot too, and they quickly identified it as well. They may have connected the recently stolen car combined with old stolen plates to the MO of the stickup men who had robbed Knight's Pharmacy less than three weeks before.

Ronnie spotted the squad car in the rear view mirror. Uh-oh, cops, he said. Roger took one look and ordered him to make a U-turn fast. Ronnie swung a two-wheeler across Lake Street, narrowly missed an oncoming car, and peeled away, weaving in and out of traffic. The cops duplicated the maneuver, lights flashing, siren howling.

Jimmy crouched in back of the steel plate with the rifle across his knees, and peeked over the top of the seat. Here they come, he yelled.

Take a right, said Roger, calmly.

They sped south on Blaisdell, with Roger leaning out the door shooting at the cops, and the cops shooting at them. The back window flew to pieces, just disintegrated. Jimmy managed to get the rifle up and fire a few wild shots. They were doing sixty-five miles an hour as they approached the intersection of 39th and Blaisdell, where the street doglegged.

Gene Reagan was watching TV in his home on Blaisdell when he heard something that might have been gunshots. He ran out to his front lawn just in time to see the Chrysler careen past, try to make the turn on 39th, and smash into a parked car. Moments later, the police skidded against the curb and almost flipped over before coming to a stop.

Reagan hit the dirt. He saw two cops emerge from the squad car directly into a hail of gunfire from two nattily dressed gunmen, who had come charging out of the Chrysler. There were dozens of shots. Bullets embedded themselves in Reagan's lawn, 350 feet away.

One officer clutched at his stomach and went down almost immediately. The other tried to get off a shot with a riot gun, but it misfired. Then he too fell to the ground. According to eyewitnesses, one of the gunmen walked calmly over to the second fallen officer, who was frantically cranking the lever of his gun, and executed him with a single shot to the head.

The two gunmen ran back to the Chrysler, and joined a third man who was behind the wheel. They tried to leave the scene, but their front fender was tangled up with the parked car they'd smashed into. The driver backed up, attempting to pull loose, and in the process ran over the surviving officer, who was trying to crawl away. They dragged him backward about twenty feet, then abandoned the Chrysler for the car it was hooked to (which presumably had the keys in it) and managed to free that car.

Reagan watched as they drove one block to a gas station, jumped out of the car they had just taken, pulled a woman who was buying gas out of her car, and took off east on 39th Street.

Mrs. Stanley McGovern, who lived closest to the scene, had been hiding under her kitchen table. Now she came out with towels to aid the fallen policemen. She found officer Robert Fossum dead from an armor-piercing .38-caliber slug through the head. Officer Ward Canfield was crumpled in the street behind the abandoned Chrysler, with a .45-caliber slug in his stomach, two broken collar- bones, a crushed chest, a fractured pelvis, a broken knee and a dislocated hip.

Mrs. McGovern didn't know what to do. She tried to clean up the carnage a little with her towels. She heard the sound of sirens getting closer.

Less than three minutes had passed since the police monitored a call from officers Fossum and Canfield, saying that they were chasing a stolen car south on Blaisdell. Then the radio had gone dead.

Moments later phone reports about the gunfight began coming in. Now squad cars and ambulances were converging on the scene from all directions.

The O'Kasicks could hear the sirens too, some from back in the direction of Lake Street, and more from the east. Roger ordered Jimmy to lie down in back because the police would be looking for three men. We'd better get a woman, he said. Look for a woman.

They spotted Mr. and Mrs. Alvin Anderson driving on 1st Avenue S. and ran them to the curb. Roger stepped out of the car waving his pistol. Get the hell out of here and get out fast, he told Mr. Anderson. You're coming with us, sister, he said to Mrs. Anderson. They pushed her into the car and left.

As soon as they turned the corner, Alvin Anderson ran to a phone booth and called the police.

Jimmy got on the floor in back, while Mrs. Anderson sat between Ronnie and Roger in front. Roger blindfolded her with her hanky, and told Jimmy to reach up and plug her ears with his fingers.

He didn't do a very good job. She told investigators that she heard "the leader" order them to "think, think, think!" She heard the one in back referred to as "Jim," and heard the driver say, "Forty-second and Second." They reeked of liquor. Sometimes they seemed to be driving fast, other times not so fast. About fifteen minutes after they kidnapped her, they ordered her out, guided her into another automobile and drove away.

A few minutes later they stopped. She heard the door open. You can leave now, the leader told her.

She heard a scraping sound as their car pulled away, but by the time she dared take the blindfold off, they were gone, leaving a smear of blue paint on the wooden garage behind 3325 Columbus Avenue S.

Officer Ward Canfield's brother, Neil, a park policeman, was one of the first to arrive at the scene of the shooting. He heard the downed officer whisper, "I can't breathe," before losing consciousness, but he didn't recognize him as his brother.

In the abandoned Chrysler police found a 30-30 Savage rifle, a paper bag containing more than 100 bullets, a receipt from the Chat 'N Nibble Drive-In, a box of armor-piercing .38 shells, three metal plates weighing more than seventy pounds each, a bag of roofing tacks, a roll of friction tape, three ticket stubs from the Hilltop Drive-In Theater, surgical bandages, a box of water-purifying tablets and a canteen of water.

A straw "boater" hat with a white band was left at the scene.

After examining those clues and listening to eyewitness descriptions, they told the press that they were looking for three smallish, flashy barroom toughs in their early twenties who bolstered their courage with liquor. They said the gunmen were part of an element in town that dressed in a certain style featuring straw hats, black shirts, white ties and dark suits with pegged pants. They considered the gunmen to be suspects in the holdup of Knight's Pharmacy on West Broadway two weeks before, and it was possible that they had been involved in other holdups as well.

They did not publicize the fact that they were looking for someone named Jim, or that they had identified the blue paint on the garage as being off a 1951 or 1952 Oldsmobile.

Robert Fossum was the best kind of police officer, the Minneapolis Star reported on August 19, a brave and fearless man who loved his work. He had three children, said the article, but only one of them was old enough to understand that daddy wasn't coming home anymore.

Fossum had recently purchased a new home for his family. His wife had a police radio set up in the basement which she often monitored to keep track of Bob, but the night of the murder she was watching TV with the kids, a Western. A news flash broke in, and that was how she found out her husband had been shot to death.

Ward Canfield was brought to Hennepin County General after the shootout and placed under twenty-four-hour-a-day armed guard. The police feared the killers would try to finish the job so he couldn't identify them. At first it was assumed that he wouldn't survive. "The gunshot alone would've killed most people," said a doctor.

Twelve days later, Canfield suddenly sat up in his hospital bed, a look of confusion on his face. He had been conscious off and on, but this was the first time he spoke. What happened? he asked officer James Funder. Why are you guarding me? I didn't do anything wrong!

Funder assured him he hadn't. I guess I've been in an accident then, Canfield said. It must have been an awful one. He spied a nurse standing in the doorway. How long have I been here? he asked. Almost two weeks, she replied. You and Mr. Fossum were chasing three boys and you were shot.

Yes, and they killed Bob! said Canfield. They didn't have to do that. Then he broke down and wept. By the time he regained his composure, a doctor and another nurse had been summoned. They ran over me, he told them. They ran over me with two cars. Bob is better off than me, he said, before losing consciousness again.

"Ward was a big, powerful man, a physical specimen," says William C. Rieman, retired, formerly a detective with the Minneapolis police. "That was what saved him. Otherwise he'd have never survived. He made medical history, had something like fourteen operations. They had to amputate his leg. He even went back to work awhile, up at the jail, but he was never the same."

Two days after the shootings the police were certain the gunmen were still in town because of the massive dragnet that had been put in place. Charles Wetherille, chief of detectives, told the Star that they were "holed up in the city or the suburbs."

The dragnet consisted of every police car in Minneapolis, two cars on loan from St. Paul, the entire state highway patrol, and several roadblocks, where hundreds of people were stopped.

Two days after the shootout, the O'Kasick brothers cashed $60 worth of bum checks at neighborhood drugstores and told their sister they were taking a construction job out of town. The next morning they got into Ronnie's blue Oldsmobile, slipped unnoticed through the massive dragnet, and headed for northern Minnesota.

The Eight-Hooter

Transcript of interrogation of James O'Kasick, Anoka County District Court:

Q: Now Jim, calling your attention to the day of August 19, 1957, what were you doing?

A: Ronald and Roger and me were together. Leaving Minneapolis.

Q: What kind of car did you have?

A: A 1952 blue Oldsmobile.

Q: When did you leave?

A: About seven or eight in the morning.

Q: Where did you go?

A: First we stopped in a swampy place near Forest Lake, then we went to Superior National Forest, that same day.

Q: What did you do when you got there?

A: Echo Trail had a lot of camping spots. We would go out on the side road where people didn't camp. We picked up groceries and a newspaper on the way. We camped and slept in the car for about a week.

One night it got chilly, down in the low forties. Ronnie was sleeping behind the wheel. He woke up shivering, and started the car to get some heat going. Jimmy was passed out next to him with a bellyful of vodka. He didn't stir, but Roger did. Roger had insomnia. He leaned up in the front seat with his pistol in his hand and asked Ronnie what was happening. I'm cold, Ronnie told him.

When the three of them talked, their conversation centered on questions of will. Would anyone believe they hadn't run over officer Canfield on purpose? Would anyone believe they hadn't set out deliberately to kill a policeman? That it had just happened?

They'd stopped talking about whether or not Roger had stood over Robert Fossum and deliberately shot him to death after Fossum's gun jammed. Eyewitness reports in the newspaper described a cold-blooded murder, but Roger denied it at first. Then he'd begun to equivocate. Maybe he did shoot the cop execution-style. What did it matter? He was dead, either way.

It mattered to Jimmy. A month later in General Hospital he asked Minneapolis police officer Buzz Winslow for the definitive answer. There is no record of Winslow's reply, but Rieman, who was an investigator on the case, says: "I'll tell you what kind of guy this one dink was, this Roger. Our officer Fossum looked him right in the eye, and said, 'please don't shoot me,' but he shot him in the head. Bam! Just like that."

Six days after they arrived on the Echo Trail, the O'Kasicks headed south again. They left on a Sunday night for the swampy area about forty miles north of the Twin Cities, where they had stopped when they first left Minneapolis. An investigator later asked Jimmy what they planned to do. He indicated that they had vague plans to pull another stickup because they were broke and hungry.

Maybe they read the Minneapolis papers and were relieved to find that they had gone from front-page headlines to oblivion, that it was no longer possible to read eyewitness accounts of the shootout, details of the investigation, lists of clues. They drove to a phone and called their younger sister, who wanted to know where they were. They just said they'd be home in a week or so.

According to Jimmy, they spent many hours discussing "this Minneapolis thing, this shooting."

They talked about surrendering but decided nobody would believe they didn't mean to do it. They wanted to go home, at least Ronnie and Jimmy did, but they couldn't, so they decided to stay put by the swamp. They slept in the car.

The sounds they heard were of cattle lowing in the distance, leaves scraping across the gravel road, poplars rattling in the wind. The dry, waist-high grass rustled when they walked through it. Mosquitoes bit them. Horseflies buzzed their ears. At first the sound of gunshots startled them, but they got used to it. It was just the farmers hunting grouse.

At night they heard the eerie cry of the bard owl, known locally as the eight-hooter, and other mysterious noises that might have been raccoons prowling their fire pit. The sounds made Jimmy wakeful. He spent many a long hour dwelling on the fate of the two policemen. Whenever he glanced at Roger, he noticed his eyes were wide open. "I don't think he ever slept," he later told investigators.

Jimmy and Ronnie didn't sleep well either. Roger made sure they were fully armed with bandoliers of ammunition under their leather Ike jackets, and they never could get comfortable.

It was damp and cool in the morning. Dew condensed on the car windows, and they got wet to the knees going out in the grass for a morning piss. The maple leaves were turning scarlet and orange. Blue meadow aster, purple thistle, golden-rod, and giant ragweed were in full bloom, but the weeds of high summer had already gone to seed, leaving lots of thorns and spiked pods that stuck to their pants.

The three of them talked about this Minneapolis thing constantly. They had made up their minds not to surrender. If they were found, yes, there would be shooting. But even if there was, they would only shoot to wound. At least Ronnie and Jimmy would only shoot to wound. Roger wasn't so sure. He might aim for the head so no one would recognize them, like he had done in Minneapolis.

Later on, Roger made another decision. I'll never be taken alive, he said.

He had some advice for Ronnie and Jimmy. If you can get away with it, just shoot to injure. But if we have to shoot our way through, shoot to kill. If you have a good chance to aim, shoot for the head.

Jimmy said, If we shoot to kill, then I'll have to be on my own. I just have to go it alone. I don't want to kill anybody else.

Shoot to kill, and stick together. That's my advice, Roger exhorted them. They just sort of left it at that.

On September 7, they were down to less than a quarter tank of gas. They searched under the seats for change and found nine cents. As dusk approached, they began looking for a place to spend the night, and came upon a little beer joint on a gravel road, right there in the middle of nowhere. Stop, said Roger.

He strolled into the bar with a pistol in his hand, and came out a few minutes later with $40 and some change.

I didn't hear any shots, said Jimmy, hopefully. I didn't have to shoot anybody, Roger replied.

They headed south and spent the night in the woods near Stillwater. The next day they stopped at a hardware store, bought some gray primer, drove into a wooded area on the bluffs outside Red Wing, and painted the car.

"We stayed around there for a few days, then drove up to Eaton's Ranch by Minneapolis, another wooded area," said Jimmy. "Many times we spent hours looking for a woods to hide in. On Friday, the 13th of September, we headed back toward Forest Lake. Back to the swamp."

Incident On Constance Road

Minneapolis Tribune: "An Anoka area ranch woman said that a friendly look and a gallon of gas could have changed the whole course of events in Saturday's death chase. Mrs. George Pantsar, Coon Creek Ranch, said a young man who would later be identified as Ronald O'Kasick walked into her yard about 5 p.m. Saturday, and asked for gas.

"I told him we didn't have any, although I really could have given him a gallon or two. I didn't like the way he looked at me. He asked several times if I was sure we didn't have any. I finally convinced him, and he left. I guess it might have changed everything if I'd given him some gas. It haunts me."

The O'Kasicks were down to their last dollar again. They were twenty miles north of the Twin Cities, heading east on Constance Road in Anoka County, looking for a store to rob, when their car ran out of gas. They rolled to a stop at an angle to the curb.

Ronnie walked down to Highway 6 and tried to bum some gas from a woman in a farmyard, but she refused, so he started hitchhiking. Mrs. Kenneth Sunderlin picked him up.

Ronnie had a disarming smile but at the same time there was something suspicious about him, Mrs. Sunderlin later told police. She was reminded, "of those drawings in the Tribune, of those killers." She dropped Ronnie off in the tiny village of Coon Rapids, then drove to the police station to tell Chief Al Bomberger about her suspicions.

Ronnie bought about a gallon of gas in a lard bucket he had picked up from a trash barrel, and started walking out of town. Anoka County Sheriff's Deputies James Sampson and Vernon Gottwald happened along. They offered to give him a lift to his car.

Ronnie had no choice. He thanked them and got in.

About that time, Mrs. Marion Lindgren and her daughter Patty, 13, were returning to their home on Constance Road. Patty's father, Eugene, had given her $10 to buy a blouse. He had closed his paint store early so he could watch the two younger kids while Patty and her mom went shopping.

Mrs. Lindgren noticed the unfamiliar gray car with its rear end protruding into the road but didn't give it much thought. She let her daughter off in front, then continued down the long driveway to the garage.

Patty ran inside to show her dad the blouse, but before she could unwrap it, Eugene Lindgren said he had a better idea. He would go out in back and work on a fence he was building, while Patty put her new blouse on. In a few minutes he would come back in to see how it looked on her.

The Lindgren's collie, Twinky, was tied up in the front yard, barking.

Jimmy took his turn hiding in the backseat and tried to get some sleep, but it was useless. Some dog kept him up with its endless barking. Roger turned on the radio and found a pop music station. Jimmy would later tell investigators that the songs reminded him of summer days driving up and down Lake Street, days when they had money to spend but hadn't murdered anybody yet. So much had happened in such a short time. Everything had changed. He finally dozed a bit.

Meanwhile, Coon Rapids Police Chief Al Bomberger and Mrs. Sunderlin were looking around for Ronnie. Mrs. Sunderlin wanted to point him out so the chief could see first-hand how suspicious he looked, but Ronnie was gone. A filling station attendant said he had sold him nineteen cents' worth of gas just minutes ago, and he had disappeared.

Deputies Sampson and Gottwald, who had picked Ronnie up, were getting suspicious too. They turned off Highway 6 onto Constance Road, and Ronnie pointed to a parked car about a hundred yards from the gray Oldsmobile and said it was his. They pulled over and let him out.

Ronnie walked to the car, slopping gas out of the bucket. He started to mess around with the gas cap, hoping the deputies would leave. They didn't, and while they were sitting there, Bernard Bass, the owner of the car, yelled from his yard, "Hey! What are you doing, that's my car."

The deputies figured they were dealing with a car thief. They got out and grabbed Ronnie. They put handcuffs on him and opened the back door. Get in, Gottwald said. They had noted the Oldsmobile parked at an odd angle down Constance Road. Now they drove up to it. Roger was sitting in the front. The officers got out of their car and approached to question him.

Jimmy was half asleep, listening to the music. He heard Roger say, "Get your gun ready, Jim," and then he heard shots.

"Roger came at those deputies like a madman, swearing and shooting, it was like he was crazy," says Rieman. A newspaper account has Roger coming at the deputies screaming and cursing and filling the air with bullets, a .38 in one hand, a .45 in the other.

Sampson was hit in the foot, but he and Gottwald both managed to reach cover around the side of a nearby house. They saw Ronnie, still handcuffed, jump out of their squad car and join Roger.

Jimmy fired two low shots from the Oldsmobile to keep the cops from shooting at Roger and Ronnie. As soon as he shot, he ran over near the squad car so the three of them were together. The deputies fired at them. Roger fired back. They ran behind a nearby house looking for a car, but there was none to be found, so they went around front again, and next door to the Lindgren home.

Jimmy saw what appeared to be two women inside. He tried the door, but it was locked. Roger headed toward the back.

As soon as Eugene Lindgren saw the gunmen in his front yard, he ran to the garage, where he kept his rifle. Lindgren was a hunter. His rifle was cleaned and ready for use, but it wasn't loaded. He got down on the floor and began crawling toward a cabinet where the bullets were kept.

Coon Rapids Police Chief Al Bomberger and Mrs. Sunderlin were still driving around looking for Ronnie when a message from Deputy Gottwald came over the radio. He and Deputy Sampson had been involved in a gunfight on Constance Road, and Sampson was wounded. Bomberger sent out an urgent bulletin to all law enforcement personnel in the area and headed for the scene.

Jimmy was still trying to get in the Lindgrens' front door when he overheard Roger back by the garage, saying, Give me the keys, we need your car! He ran around the house and saw a man lying on the garage floor next to a rifle. Jimmy picked the rifle up, realized it was empty, and put it aside.

Lindgren's red and white Cadillac was still warm. Roger told Lindgren to get in, drive, and do exactly what he was told. He sat in the front seat next to Lindgren and held his .45 to the hostage's head. Ronnie and Jimmy got in back. Ronnie was still handcuffed.

They backed out of the driveway and headed east on Constance Road, toward the Carlos Avery Game Farm.

Gottwald and Sampson didn't shoot, or follow. They waited until the Cadillac was well down the road before they emerged and sent out a radio report. It included a description of the gunmen, the color, make, and year of the Lindgrens' car, and the direction it was traveling.

Moments later Chief Bomberger screeched to a stop in front of the Lindgren home. Marion Lindgren was out in front. "My husband is in that car," she shouted.

"The look of terror on that woman's face was pitiful," Bomberger told reporters.

The radio was still playing in the Oldsmobile parked on Constance Road.

Fugue

Minneapolis Tribune, September 16, 1957: "Joyce O'Ka-sick had a dream. She was 22 and in Shakopee prison at the time. In her dream she saw her dead mother with Ronnie. 'I woke up scared. I knew something terrible would happen,' she said.

"The next day, Saturday, about four in the afternoon, she be-gan writing a letter to Jimmy. Then, instead of finishing it she walked over to the prison laundry, sneaked out the back door, and ran across a field before the guard could spot her. She had escaped. She had to find her brothers."

At that very moment her brothers were heading down a gravel road ninety-five miles an hour in a stolen Cadillac, with a hostage at the wheel.

Rocks smacked the underside of the car and rattled off the oil pan. Jimmy retreated to the farthest side of the backseat and plugged his ears. Roger leaned over from the front, put the muzzle of his gun to the links of Ronnie's handcuffs, and blew them apart. BAM! The Cadillac filled with gun smoke.

The hostage was plenty scared. He told Roger to be careful. Just drive, Roger said, and drive fast. Roger was very cool and calm. He told the hostage that he was riding with the cop-killers from Minneapolis, and he'd better do what he was told if he wanted to survive.

I've got a wife and kids, the hostage said.

Me too, Ronnie told him. I've got a wife and kids.

Roger gave Ronnie his .45 because they had left Ronnie's pistol in the Oldsmobile. There were four rounds gone, so Ronnie dumped the magazine and reloaded. They had plenty of ammunition.

They saw a police car ahead on the left side of the road, and two policemen with rifles standing behind it. Get down, Roger ordered, but there wasn't any room on the floor, and they were approaching fast, so Jimmy and Ronnie had to sit up.

Tell the cops not to shoot, roll down your window! Roger said to the hostage.

They roared right by with Lindgren yelling, HOSTAGE! DON'T SHOOT!

If Jimmy looked low under the dust plume they were raising, he could see a police car behind them, red lights flashing. They came to an intersection with a road going south, and they took it. That was a mistake. It led directly to the little village of Forest Lake. They sped three blocks down the main street, then doubled back, somehow losing the police car in the process. They got back on the gravel road again, and took off in the direction they had just come from. Roger saw a plane overhead.

Keep going, step on it, he told the hostage.

About a minute later the car sputtered to a stop. Get it moving, Roger ordered.

It wouldn't start. The hostage tried pumping the accelerator and pulling the choke. Nothing. They got out and looked at the plane circling overhead. Roger said they should make a run for some trees about a hundred feet down the road on their right. He grabbed the hostage by the arm and stayed in the rear. Jimmy led the way. When they glanced over their shoulders, they could see dust rising on the road behind them, and they knew what was coming.

Highway patrolmen James Crawford and Kenneth Cziok (pronounced Chuck) had been in separate cars when the report about the incident on Constance Road came over the wire.

Crawford almost caught up to the Cadillac in Forest Lake, but his brakes failed when he tried to double back. Moments later Cziok arrived and Crawford got in his car. The pictures that appeared in newspapers the next day created the impression that a massive posse was involved in the chase, but that was a misconception.

"There were two cars at first, then we had the one car," Crawford explains. "All those people you see in the pictures arrived after the shooting was over. Kenny Cziok and I chased them, with the help of the airplane."

Minutes after Crawford jumped into Cziok's car, the pilot told them that the Cadillac had stopped in a ditch on the Carlos Avery Game Farm. "He told us that four people got out," says Crawford. "He said two of them were close together near the car, and the others had run down the road. We pulled up right behind the car, and I saw two individuals in the road. One of them had a gun to the head of the other one. Kenny took his pistol and jumped out the driver's side. I left mine on the seat and grabbed the shotgun.

"I advanced, they backed off, and we went maybe twenty-five yards down the road that way."

The Sheriff

The O'Kasicks were stickup men and killers who committed at least fifteen armed robberies, stole more than $20,000, and gathered an arsenal of deadly weapons that they used with reckless disregard in three shoot-outs with the police. They dressed in the gangster style of their day to signify the status they craved. Their crimes, though carefully planned, were increasingly reckless and brazen. They wanted to be outlaws and outlaws they were, but when they met James Crawford they met the Sheriff. The movie was over.

When the patrol car pulled up behind them, Roger and the hostage had made it nearly to a thicket, with Ronnie and Jimmy about fifty feet ahead. Two officers jumped out, one holding a shotgun. A pistol shot zinged over their heads.

Don't turn around, Roger told his brothers calmly. Just run to the swamp on the other side of that brush as quick as you can.

Crawford advanced to within ten feet of Roger and the hostage. Ronnie and Jimmy crouched half hidden in the bushes, their guns drawn.

Roger positioned the hostage facing him, with his back to the shotgun. He held Lindgren by the collar behind the neck with his left hand, shoved the barrel of his pistol up under his chin with his right hand, and made a move toward the patrolman.

Crawford didn't flinch.

"HOSTAGE, FALL DOWN!" he commanded.

"Stand still," said Roger quietly. "Do what I say."

Lindgren looked back over his shoulder at the officer, then at Roger. He didn't know what to do. There was a pistol crack, then a thunderous blast.

"The gunman tripped, or maybe the hostage tripped, but both of them went down," says Crawford. "There was a shot, then the one with the gun got up. I fired at him, he dropped in the brush, and I fired again where he'd fallen because his gun was still going off."

Roger O'Kasick had checked out the way he would have scripted it, an automatic weapon jerking his dead hand, his finger squeezed on the trigger, blazing away at a cop. A bullet went through Crawford's pants leg.

"I saw the other two individuals rising up from where they'd ducked," says Crawford. "One of them pointed his weapon at me, and I shot him too."

Jimmy hugged the ground, momentarily deafened by the blasts. He caught a glimpse of Roger down in the weeds, smoke rising from the ragged holes in his buckshot-riddled Ike jacket. Ronnie was nearby, choking and coughing up blood. He bolted toward Ronnie, wondering as he ran why nobody shot him. Ronnie's eyelids fluttered. He tried to say something. Then his eyes rolled back.

Jimmy thought he should die too, that they should all die together. He saw a patch of high weeds and ran for it so he could have a few moments to think.

The first thing he did was open his .38 and let two empty casings fall out, along with the live ammunition. Then he re-loaded carefully. He didn't want the gun to jam when he killed himself. He was concerned about the hostage, he later told police. He wondered where Lindgren was.

Lindgren was dead. Roger shot him through the neck as they fell.

Jimmy crouched in the weeds. He was just about ready to charge out and go down trying to avenge his dead broth-ers when it occurred to him that there was nothing to avenge. His brothers were dead because they were ready to die, because they preferred death to surrender. He didn't know which of those he preferred, so he flattened himself in the weeds.

He saw the plane circling and knew the pilot must be able to see him. It wasn't dark yet, but the crickets had begun to chirp. They were down so low they thought it was night. And he was right there with them.

Hours passed before he heard car doors slamming and the sound of voices all around, as if an army were gathering and coming closer.

He put the gun to his head, but he couldn't bring himself to pull the trigger. They were just a few feet away. He held the gun to where he thought his heart was and fired. Someone said, "There he is, he shot himself." Another voice said, "Fill him full of holes."

He felt a foot on his back, and someone ordered him to slide the gun out from under himself. Then he was in an ambulance.

Postmortems

Eugene Lindgren was born in the Anoka area, and lived there all his life. He had a wife, three children, a thriving business, a red and white Cadillac, and a new home on Constance Road. He was thirty years old when the O'Kasicks happened to him.

Lindgren's wife was in a state of paralyzing grief and shock for a few days after her husband's death. Patty did most of the talking. "Dad saved our lives," she said. "They would have broken down the door and taken us if he hadn't run for the gun."

Ronald O'Kasick had an inferiority complex, probably due to his size, according to psychological tests administered when he was in St. Cloud prison. He also had a speech defect that he covered by mumbling. He thought most people were "two-faced." He hated his father, and looked to his older brother Roger for guidance.

A week before the murder of officer Robert Fossum, Ronnie had visited his ex-wife and two children. He promised to come back in a few days, but they never saw him again. His ex-wife said that everything seemed OK in their relationship until Roger came around. "He would just start something between us and take Ronnie away for the rest of the night. As soon as Roger arrived everything got all hush-hush, and secret."

Roger was bitter with life, according to his sister Joyce. "I've never seen a guy with so much misery in him. He never hung around with other guys. He liked girls, but he only had a couple dates in his life and he was good looking too. My girlfriends thought so. I remember when I told him how Jerry's (her fiancé's) friend had been shot and paralyzed by the cops, he had tears in his eyes and he swore at the cops. Over someone he didn't even know. He was smart in school, a lot smarter than the rest of us. He hated to go to school though, because he didn't have the right clothes and other kids laughed at him. He hated people. He'd think too much. I guess you could say he had an inferiority complex or something."

Roger had worked in factories a few weeks at a time for a total of less than six months. What he liked to do was sit in his rented room and read library books.

Around midnight September 14, a few hours after the first news reports of the Anoka County shootout began coming in and the first pictures of the dead bodies appeared on Twin Cities TV screens, the police received a tip that Joyce O'Kasick, who had escaped from Shakopee Prison that afternoon, could be found at the Dugout Bar in downtown Minneapolis.

When the police arrived, Joyce ran out the back door and tried to hide in a parked car. The officers approached cautiously, guns drawn, and threw the doors open. "Why don't you just kill me like you killed my brothers, you dirty coppers," Joyce sobbed.

Jimmy had nicked his heart when he shot himself. His lung collapsed, and a tracheotomy tube was pushed down his throat in the ambulance. By the time he reached General Hospital in Minneapolis he was stable, but a few hours later he turned blue from the waist up and went into shock. An emergency operation was performed and 10 stitches were sewn into a major heart muscle. His heart never worked right after that, and he tired easily.

Shortly after the operation, while he was still groggy, the police began taking statements from him, and continued doing so for the next three weeks. He confessed to shooting officer Ward Canfield in the stomach at point blank range, and said that Roger, who was "criminally insane, someone I never knew," murdered officer Bob Fossum. He said that running over Canfield and shooting the hostage Eugene Lindgren were both accidents. He told of armed robberies he'd participated in since his discharge from the Marines, and was able to provide details of his brother's career as holdup men for the previous two years.

Jimmy's interest in life waxed and waned during his confinement. He and his brother Richard convinced themselves that Lindgren was actually shot by patrolman Crawford, and both of them spent a lot of energy trying to convince others of their theory. That hyped him awhile, even though their efforts proved fruitless. He was quickly convicted of second degree murder for the Minneapolis shootout, and first degree murder for the death of Eugene Lindgren. The sentences were imposed consecutively, which left him no hope of ever getting out of prison and threw him into a permanent state of depression. Jerry Roy, a friend of his from the Franklin Avenue days, says he attempted suicide several times at St. Cloud prison. "That last time they just did him a favor and let him bleed for a while before they called the ambulance," Roy says. "He wanted to die real bad."

James Crawford had a long and varied career after he shot the O'Kasicks. He headed the state highway patrol, served as state registrar, and then went to Saudi Arabia, where he set up a system of outposts and surveillance in that country's remote borderlands. After he returned, he was elected mayor of Forest Lake. September 14, 1957, was surely one of the pivotal points of his life, but when he recalls that day, he doesn't think so much of the danger he faced, or the adrenalin-pumping drama. The texture of the moments as they passed is what sticks with him—the way the ankle-deep water in the grass squished in his shoes, the eerie quiet that descended after the shooting was over, the sound of the eight-hooter owl, and how cold his feet got as dusk settled in and he and his partner waited behind their car for backup.

"We'd been ordered not to go in after that third guy until help arrived, but it took a long time," he says.

Highway patrolmen, police from nearby jurisdictions, and local farmers who just grabbed their rifles and joined the posse had been quickly organized, but they were confused about where to go.

"They'd been told to look for the airplane," Crawford explains. "Our plane was circling over the area, but one of the sheriffs sent up another plane. As soon as it got to the scene our pilot told him to get out of there because he was busy watching the ground, and he didn't want to worry about crashing into him. So the second plane went and circled over Coon

Lake, and that's where all the backup went. It took a long time to straighten that out."

Queried if there was any way the hostage might have been saved, Crawford says maybe. "If I'd have shot before the two of them fell I might have managed to hit the O'Kasick kid without harming that poor fellow. But it seemed an awful chance to take."

Decades after their crimes, the O'Kasicks' trail is marked by missing files and blank stares. One of the few cops who agreed to talk about them was retired detective Rieman. "The nurses at General Hospital treated that kid pretty special," he said of Jimmy. "They babied him. Of course he was a celebrity."

According to newspaper accounts, investigators interrogated Jimmy for more than twenty hours during his three-week hospital stay, but quotes in the newspapers and a few pages of transcript labeled "Dying Declaration James O'Kasick" are all that survive. The rest, more than one hundred pages, have disappeared. Rieman hinted that they were deliberately destroyed.

"Kid made excuses," he said, "whined about his rotten life, claimed they were always broke and hungry, said the old man had them boosting car parts and selling them down at the junkyards when they were ten years old." He sighed, as if to say that there is no end to human gullibility. His attitude implied a question: Why are you writing about them?

"Remember anything else about the O'Kasick case?" I asked, hoping he would say, no, and the interview would be over.

He corrected my query. "You mean the Fossum-Canfield case. The murder of Minneapolis police officer Robert Fossum, and the attempted murder of officer Ward Canfield."

Just stating those facts was an emotional effort for him. His face flushed, but he continued.

"They shot the handcuffs off that one kid while they were going ninety-five miles an hour on a dirt road. Do you know how crazy that is? Put a hole right through the gas tank, that's why the car quit on them. They were murderers, vicious little dinks, but I'll tell you something. They didn't kill that hostage on purpose."

Rieman has deduced this as follows: "There was no post-mortem. Usually there is, you know, but it should have been done in Anoka, and instead they sent the bodies to Minneapolis because nobody knew what to do out there." He shook his head. "God, it was a mess. Anyway, my partner and I had to view the bodies at the morgue, and this Roger O'Kasick's finger on his left hand, his index finger, was taped together at the knuckle. It had been shot in half. Stand up here once," he said.

Rieman came out from behind the desk.

"Now Roger had the hostage like this." He looped his left hand behind my head and jerked me toward him. "And he was leading him along, stepping backwards with his pistol shoved up under the hostage's chin, like this." He jabbed a finger into my neck.

"Now Roger, he must have stumbled as he stepped backwards in the weeds, and his gun fired, shot the hostage through the neck, and blew his own finger off. And then, of course, that highway patrolman shot him. Shot him dead."

Rieman sat back in his swivel chair and nodded, folding his hands in front of him, big powerful hands, with fingers the size of midget bananas, one of which was missing at the middle knuckle. He smiled an enigmatic little smile.

"Now what was that patrolman's name? Crawford, I think."

The Milwaukee Avenue Massacre

The Milwaukee Avenue Massacre

In the preceding story I mentioned that the O'Kasick gang was on their way to rob a Red Owl supermarket when their shootout with the Minneapolis police occurred. A short time after the story came out, I was contacted by Bill Cooley, a wealthy man who later served as Mayor of a Twin Cities suburb. He said he'd read the story with special interest, because he was working as a carry-out boy at Red Owl that day. Cooley asked me if I wanted to go to Chicago and write about a fight he was promoting, former heavyweight champion Joe Frazier's comeback bout.

I agreed, but it wasn't much of a fight. Frazier made such a mediocre showing that he re-retired. The hype that preceded the bout didn't have much story potential either, but while I was in Chicago a quadruple murder on the northwest side made headlines, so I went to the scene just to poke around. All I managed to discover was that virtually an entire Mexican town had emptied out and moved into the building where the crime took place.

Eight years later I got a chance to pitch a story to Chicago Magazine. I asked if they were interested in the dynamics of a building in Chicago that housed most of the former residents of a Mexican town, with all its history and quirks. They were, so I proceeded by contacting the men who'd been convicted of the murders, and asking them if they wanted to talk. The only one who spoke English, Rogelio Arroyo, said he'd be glad to. When I went to Pontiac Prison to interview him, his first words were, "I'm innocent. All four of us are innocent. For God's sake get us out of here."

I was skeptical, but when I went to where the murders occurred again, and talked to people there, it became apparent that it was common knowledge that the wrong men had been convicted. I enlisted the aid of Margo De Ley, a teacher at the University of Illinois Chicago who spoke fluent Spanish, and we researched the case together for about a month. That was the story I turned in to Chicago Magazine. It wasn't what they were expecting, but to their credit they accepted it, and made it their cover story in May 1990.

"I was pulling off my raincoat when the phone rang," says Margo De Ley." As soon as I heard who it was, I ran upstairs and grabbed my landlord so that he could be a witness."

Her landlord is a lawyer, and the man on the phone was calling to confess to murder.

The caller, Gilberto Varela, spent the next half hour recounting the details of one of the more stunning multiple murders to occur in Chicago in the eighties, the stuff of bad movies and urban nightmares. Also, according to Varela's description, it was a completely different crime than the one that Chicago police investigators claimed they had solved, and for which a judge and jury had convicted four Mexican defendants eight years ago.

"Those men now in prison for the murders," said Varela, "none of them was there. I was there."

Although it happened on the near northwest side, the crime to which Varela admitted was barely a Chicago murder at all. On Thanksgiving Day 1981, four undocumented workers were gunned down, victims of a family feud that had followed them from the town of Acupetlahuaya, in the Mexican state of Guerrero. One lawyer called it "the Mexican version of the Hatfields and the McCoys."

Four Mexican men—Rogelio Arroyo, Ignacio Varela, Isauro Sanchez and Joaquin Varela, all illegal immigrants—were arrested immediately. None of them spoke English. They were scared of deportation, of the police, of the courts. They barely understood what was happening. Within months of their arrest, they were sentenced to natural life in prison for a crime they didn't commit.

"People who were born and raised here are sometimes overwhelmed by the justice system," says De Ley. "Imagine what it must be like when you don't speak the language, when you have to rely on an interpreter who works for the courts or the police to tell your story."

Or, as one eyewitness to the murders, who refused to allow his name to be used, says: "If this was Mexico, the men could have told their stories, which made perfect sense, in their own words, as soon as they were arrested. They wouldn't have had to do it through a translator, days later, after things had become hopeless…"

The Meat Industry

It's a warm autumn day, and the street where the four victims died is bustling. The sugary smell of deep-fried sweet breads drifts down Milwaukee Avenue from the Estrella de Oro bakery. Ranchero music blares from the International Records store. "Tamales! Tamales!" cries an elderly woman peddling food from a cart. At Teatro Vicente Hernandez (the Mexican theater), a movie called Las Ruleteras (The Lady Cab Drivers) is playing. A knot of young boys stands ogling the poster featuring senoritas in short shorts, T-shirts, and cabbies' hats.

Just up the street is the site of the murders, 2121 North Milwaukee Avenue, a squat, gloomy-looking place that fills most of a city block. Once it was all Polish residents, but now it's "100 percent Mexican," says building superintendent Arturo Cabrera. "Most new tenants are recommended by people who live here. People know about this building back in Mexico, so they look for me when they first come to Chicago. They like the neighborhood. It's just like home."

Home for most of them is Guerrero. Chicago has been a magnet for people from Guerrero for generations, because they are superb hog butchers. The ability to reduce a 400 pound pig to a few bones and a memory in a matter of minutes is a test of manhood for Guerrerenos, and nothing goes to waste. Blood and guts become fertilizer. Ears are deep-fried and eaten like potato chips. The head, hooves, and tail are used in pozole, Guerrereno soul food.

In the twenties and thirties, when the meat-packing industry was in full swing, Guerrerenos could find well-paid work in Chicago. Today, they still come to find work in the packing houses, paying large fees, often their life savings, to "coyotes" who shepherd them across the border. There, the proverbial good and bad news awaits them. The good news is, there is still a meat industry in Chicago. The bad news is, they are the meat. Instead of finding nasty but well-paid work butchering hogs, they find nasty, low-paid work as janitors, car washers, factory workers and temp laborers.

"They eat you alive here," says Tonio, an undocumented worker living in Bucktown, who explains that the minimum wage is on the high end of the pay scale for many of his countrymen. Some work for as little as $1.50 an hour. Others are routinely cheated out of their paychecks because employers know they have no legal recourse.

The results can be seen at 2121 North Milwaukee, a rabbit warren of a building where the tiny apartments are often shared by five or more tenants. "Five people working for three dollars an hour," building superintendent Cabrera says, "that's $15 an hour, and that's how my countrymen survive."

The men who died on Thanksgiving Day 1981 all came from Guerrero. So did the men who went to prison for killing them, as well as the actual killers. Things in Chicago didn't work out as any of them had hoped.

Rogelio Arroyo was the first to arrive, having paid a coyote $500 to smuggle him over the border in 1979. He was 24 years old, soft-spoken, without English skills or work papers. He quickly found work as a house painter, but before long pulled himself up to the four dollar an hour level by landing a job making steel cabinets and dog cages.

"There were lots of illegals working at that factory," he says. "That was my life, working."

His wife, who had stayed behind in Mexico, soon joined him, leaving their two children with her parents. The couple did what many new Mexican arrivals do. They moved in with relatives who'd preceded them to Chicago. They started sharing a Bucktown apartment with Gilberto Varela, a cousin of Rogelio Arroyo's wife.

The apartment was crowded, Arroyo remembers, especially after both his wife and Gilberto's had babies, but family ties are strong among people from rural Mexico, and family ties soon packed the apartment. By the fall of 1981, Ignacio Varela—known to one and all as "Uncle Nacho"—had moved in. A sociable, easygoing man, Uncle Nacho embarked on a daily regimen of half-hearted job hunting and enthusiastic beer drinking. Along with him came his brother Ramiro Varela, 32, a more intense man and a harder drinker.

By November 1981, life for all of them had settled into a routine. The men worked, made little money, and drove around listening to ranchero music at night. The wives held jobs, fussed over the babies, cooked. None of them spoke any English except for Gilberto, and his was choppy. They didn't leave the neighborhood except to go to work.

"It wasn't much fun," remembers Arroyo, "but it was a way to live. We just wanted to save some money and go back to Mexico."

The Milwaukee Avenue Massacre

"Four Charged in Ambush," reads a Sun-Times, front page headline about the shootings. "The six victims, who were not armed, were leaving the apartment building at 2121 North Milwaukee about 11:30 p.m. Thursday when they were shot at close range... The shooting stemmed from a family feud that began in Mexico."

Later reports called it, "The Milwaukee Avenue Massacre."

The police had learned to expect trouble in Bucktown on Thanksgiving, a holiday that means little in immigrant communities except a late night followed by a day off. But the cops were not prepared for the scene that greeted them when they responded to reports of guns being fired at 2121 North Milwaukee. It was almost surreal.

The smell of pozole wafted through the air. Ranchero music blared from windows a few floors above where parties were still in progress, the party-goers unaware of the horrific crime that had taken place below. Down on the street a crowd, almost none of whom spoke English, many of whom were staggering drunk, milled around the building entrance where the bodies still lay. Few would give their names or a statement. Women were screaming, men were swearing revenge. The sidewalk was awash with blood.

The entrance to the building was blocked by the dead. The first of the doomed men had been shot in the foyer, stumbled out to the sidewalk, turned back, maybe to help those still inside. Falling to his knees, he'd crawled toward the entrance and died with his head in the doorway.

Halfway up the front staircase, another man lay dead. A third had bled to death in the vestibule. The last man, who ran from the scene shouting for help, was chased down and shot to death half a block away.

Two other men had been wounded, one superficially, one critically. Both were still near the building when police arrived. They were dispatched to St. Elizabeth's Hospital, together with officers to take their statements.

Difficult as it was to get a straightforward explanation of what happened, the police did finally determine two things: all but one of the murdered men were part of the Sanchez family; and each of the killers was said to be part of another family, the Varelas.

"Gilberto Varela" was a name investigators at the scene heard several times, first from one of the wounded men, an undocumented worker named Rogelio Medina, then from the other surviving victim, 25-year-old Leoncio Quezada, who was lapsing in and out of shock. According to police reports, Quezada was not only wounded, he was extremely drunk. All the murderers were Varelas, he mumbled in broken English.

The motive, as far as the police could determine, seemed to be a blood feud that began years earlier, when a twenty-something Varela man ran off with his cousin, a 13-year-old Sanchez girl. Her family tracked them down and forced the girl to come home. Her lover let her go, but swore that the Sanchez family would pay. Less than a year later, there was a gunfight in Acupetlahuaya. When it was over, a Varela was wounded and a Sanchez was dead. Bad blood between the two families escalated from there, even though they continued to intermarry, and often changed sides for a variety of reasons.

The Bucktown neighborhood harbored many Sanchezes and Varelas. People named Sanchez and Varela were cousins, spouses, and in-laws to one another. In fights, which were frequent, some Varelas sided with the Sanchezes, some Sanchezes with the Varelas. But the police, in the confusion and bloodiness of that Thanksgiving night in Bucktown, understood only that families named Sanchez and Varela feuded, that some Sanchez men were dead, and that there was a houseful of Varelas, including Gilberto Varela, the man whom several witnesses had fingered, living nearby.

They went to Gilberto's apartment, but arrested Rogelio Arroyo instead.

Pozole

Thanksgiving night at the apartment had started quietly. "My wife and I went to a movie at the Mexican Theatre," Arroyo says. When they returned, Gilberto was listening to music. Ramiro and Uncle Nacho were drinking beer. They'd been through a couple six-packs. Nacho soon fell asleep.

Arroyo's wife started cooking, while Arroyo sat in the living room, zoned out the music and let the pungent smell of the pozole she was preparing work its spell. He says he daydreamed of home, and contemplated the taste of that first savory spoonful of pozole. But it never came.

The telephone rang. Gilberto Varela answered. "The murders wouldn't have happened," says Arroyo's wife, "except for that call."

On the other end was Saul Varela, yet another uncle of Gilberto's. Uncle Saul's marital troubles had been the subject of jokes in the Arroyo/Varela household for months. Saul and his wife had just moved into 2121 North Milwaukee, having abruptly left the apartment they'd been sharing with another man, Rogelio Medina. Saul told Gilberto that Medina, a buddy of many Chicago Sanchezes, had been sleeping with his wife. He was sure of it.

Medina and several friends, including three Sanchezes, had shown up at 2121 North Milwaukee that night, hoping to find a party. What they found first was Saul Varela, wandering in the hallway. According to neighbors, a fight erupted and Saul ran for his apartment with the Sanchezes chasing him, swearing and hollering. As they began kicking at his door, Saul scurried out the window, down the fire escape, and up the street to a pay phone, where he called Gilberto.

"Gilberto talked to him for a minute and hung up," remembers Arroyo. "He told us Saul needed help, and asked Ramiro to come with him. They put on their jackets, and they got their pistols, too. Did they know there would be shooting? I think it was just a precaution, you know, because it was the Sanchezes and the Varelas."

Gilberto and Ramiro then did something they'd done often before. They called their 16-year-old-cousin Joaquin for a ride.

Joaquin, who'd left Mexico two years earlier, was small and shy in a community where machismo was highly valued. So as soon as he saved up some money he bought a shiny, souped-up Chevy. Ever since, he had eagerly offered rides to his older cousins Gilberto and Ramiro.

"He was practically their chauffeur," says Arroyo. His cousins urged him to get a pistol so he could take care of himself, and he did.

Joaquin drove Gilberto and Ramiro to 2121 North Milwaukee that night. He admits he had a pistol. But he insists he dropped his passengers off, then parked a block up the street and waited.

Gilberto and Ramiro met uncle Saul near the building. There, they were joined by a fourth man Saul had recruited,

Irineo Trujillo. The four walked into the entryway of the 2121 building and spotted Medina coming downstairs.

Gilberto pointed his pistol at him and shouted, "time to settle accounts!"

Medina, who had a knife, lunged at Gilberto. The gun went off, striking Medina in the leg, and all hell broke loose.

"Gilberto wasn't gone more than 20 minutes," says Arroyo. "He came back bleeding from a knife wound in the arm. 'I really messed up,' he said. 'I shot some people. I just went crazy and emptied the gun. I think maybe two Sanchezes are dead.' Then he left."

Not long afterward, Gilberto called the apartment and talked to his wife. "She woke up Uncle Nacho, grabbed the baby, and they left too," Arroyo says. "I don't know where they went. Not with Gilberto."

Within hours, Gilberto Varela, Ramiro Varela, Saul Varela and Irineo Trujillo had departed Chicago. Late the next day they crossed the border into Mexico.

At the apartment, turmoil reigned. Arroyo's wife was frightened and wanted to leave, but Arroyo wanted to stay put, adamant that he'd done nothing to make him run. "But my wife said she knew the Sanchez family well, and she thought that soon they'd come looking for revenge." So the two of them went to stay with one of Arroyo's wife's uncles.

The next morning, Friday, November 27th, Arroyo's wife went back to the apartment to pack some clothes. The police were waiting for her. She broke down and wept, recalling the interrogation.

She soon told police where her husband was. "Then they tried to make me say things I didn't mean," she said. "We had nothing to hide. Rogelio was right in front of my eyes when the crime took place. After they arrested him this one officer who spoke Spanish looked right at me and said, 'Lady, you told me your husband had gone there to 2121 North Milwaukee.' I never said that at all, but he kept saying I did. That's a lie!"

A few hours after being detained, Arroyo's wife gave a statement in Spanish to a police interpreter. She chose her words carefully. But when the transcript was handed to her, it was written in English. She had no idea what the document said.

"They told me to sign it and I did," she says. "I was terrified."

One thing that police didn't make clear to her was who they thought she was, Mrs. Gilberto Varela. While she was still at the police station investigators arrested her husband, Rogelio Arroyo, under Gilberto's name. The confusion was cleared up only after Arroyo had been in jail for more than 24 hours. The police simply crossed out Gilberto's name and substituted Arroyo's.

Meanwhile, Uncle Nacho and Joaquin Varela were arrested at the staked-out apartment, Joaquin with a pistol in his pocket. Before they could be transported to Cook County Jail another relative drove up, unluckily.

Isauro Sanchez, 26, was a nephew to Uncle Nacho, cousin to Gilberto, and a brother of Rogelio Arroyo's wife. He was a hardworking husband and father who'd never been in any trouble in Chicago. He was driving Gilberto's wife back to her apartment so she could get some clothes and money when he was arrested, and ultimately charged with four counts of murder.

By late Friday afternoon the investigators felt their efforts had been very successful, and even had a certain symmetry.

Four Mexicans were dead, and four Mexicans were in custody for murder. All that remained was getting the men to confess. But they wouldn't.

They were held separately, and not allowed to communicate. They were not even officially charged until the following Monday, and until then they couldn't get anyone to tell them why they were being held.

"Some of the police spoke Spanish," says Arroyo, "but I was confused. How was I going to be arrested for something I didn't do? How was this possible? They kept saying that the others had already confessed and that they'd said I was there, so I should confess, too."

Arroyo's family hired a lawyer who came to the station shortly after his arrest, but the other men had no counsel. Their Miranda rights had been read to them in Spanish, and they'd said they understood. They didn't request a lawyer.

"The correct procedures may have been followed, but that doesn't mean the system served these men well," says Margo De Ley. "Most immigrants are frightened of American institutions to begin with because they don't know how things work, and they never completely understand what's happening to them if they get sucked into the system."

Eyewitnesses to the event seem to have been similarly cowed. Although research for this article revealed that it was common knowledge in Bucktown that the wrong men had been arrested, no one came forward when it could have made a difference. "They were afraid of the police, of being deported, of the relatives of both families, and just of getting involved," De Ley says. "You can hardly blame them. Imagine how terrified Americans are of landing in a Mexican jail. It's the same for Mexicans here."

After almost three days of questioning their suspects, the police had a breakthrough. Joaquin's interrogator told him (falsely, in Spanish), "Your friends say they weren't at the scene, but they saw you there."

Joaquin replied: "Si ellos dicen yo estuve alla, ellos estuvieron alla tambien entonces" (If they say I was there, then they must have been there, too). The police seized on the remark, claiming that it was not only an admission that Joaquin was present when the murders took place, but it implicated the other men as well.

Joaquin later recanted the statement, saying it had been purely rhetorical. But he compounded the damage with an amended statement. In it, he admitted he drove to Milwaukee Avenue. The police demanded that he say the other accused men were with him. Eventually he did, sort of, telling an officer that Uncle Nacho had gone with him in the car, and that he'd seen Isauro Sanchez and Arroyo at the scene as well. No one asked him how he could have seen them in front of 2121 Milwaukee if his car was parked up the block. He told them he "heard shooting," and had even shot wildly twice himself, thinking that someone was chasing him.

Life Without Parole

Joaquin's statement may have doomed all of the men. It certainly contributed to the chaos at the strange legal proceeding that followed eight months later. For Arroyo, the catastrophe that his trial was to become was foreshadowed by what happened two weeks before it began, when his lawyer died.

"It was a heart attack, nothing sinister," says Daniel E. Radakovich, appointed by the judge to represent Arroyo because his family couldn't afford to hire another lawyer. "The problem was, it left us so little time to prepare."

The greater problem lay with Joaquin. By the time the trial began he was saying he wanted to retract his confession, claiming he'd been pressured by police to implicate the other three defendants. His lawyer, Andrea Lyon, fought to have the confession suppressed, but the judge ruled that it could be entered. Faced with this setback, and believing it might indicate a certain predisposition on the part of the judge, Lyon instructed her client to request a jury trial.

The other three men were advised by their attorneys to seek a bench trial. "We were convinced that the evidence against our guys was so weak that a judge would have to find them innocent," says Radakovich. "Juries, on the other hand, can be capricious. They hear a story about this horrific killing, Hispanic men gunning one another down on the streets of Chicago, and there may be an inclination to convict. I don't mean to imply that there'd be overt prejudice, but these things can be insidious."

So Arroyo, Uncle Nacho, and Isauro Sanchez opted for a bench trial.

As a result, the four defendants ran head-on into one of the quirks of the U.S. legal system. When two separate trials involve the same evidence, they are frequently held together for reasons of judicial economy. Police and eyewitnesses have to be called only once. The jury is dismissed if the testimony doesn't concern their case, but the judge hears all the testimony and has the difficult task of ignoring any evidence that is not officially part of the bench trial. Joaquin's statement, for example.

"You can't have co-defendants testifying against one another," says Radakovich. "So what Joaquin said should have played no part in the judge's verdict in Arroyo's case, or in the case of the other two men. The prosecution's whole case technically rested on the testimony of Leoncio Quezada."

In fact, Leoncio Quezada, the man who'd been shot and critically wounded, was the only eyewitness who testified at the trial. The other survivor, Rogelio Medina, who'd also named Gilberto Varela as his assailant, headed for Mexico as soon as he had recovered enough to travel, and not long afterward died there without ever naming any other of the killers.

The prosecution's case against Arroyo, Uncle Nacho, and Isauro Sanchez rested solely on the shoulders of Quezada, even though on the night of Thanksgiving 1981, Quezada made a very unreliable witness.

"The guy was absolutely dead drunk when he was shot," says Radakovich. "All of the victims were. When we saw their blood-alcohol levels, we actually thought about bringing up the cause of death question. I mean, these guys were almost dead from alcohol poisoning."

The prosecution admitted that Quezada had had a blood-alcohol reading well above the level at which someone is legally drunk in Illinois. He also had been shot in the stomach. But before the trial, while he was still in the intensive-care unit, after having been awakened by police investigators on several occasions, he identified snapshots of Gilberto Varela, Ramiro Varela, and each of the men on trial. (Operating without a search warrant, the police had gotten the photographs from Gilberto and Arroyo's apartment.) With a hospital orderly acting as translator, the police had gotten a statement from Quezada in which he said he knew each of the men in the photos personally.

Once on the stand, Quezada stuck by his statement. However, he had some difficulty under cross-examination. He admitted, for one thing, that he had seen Ignacio Varela only once before, 17 years earlier in Mexico, and he'd also seen Arroyo only once before, in a crowded department store about a year previous to the crime. He testified at one point that he saw Isauro Sanchez with a gun, later that he did not. His testimony about Joaquin was inconsistent as well. At one point, he testified that he had never seen the boy shoot a gun. Another time, Quezada stated, "I think he tried to shoot." A third time, Quezada said Joaquin did shoot that night.

There were 56 bullets, casings, or other ballistic evidence found at the murder site. Forensics experts determined that none of the bullets were fired from the gun Joaquin was carrying when he was arrested.

"There's just no way that Arroyo or the others should have been convicted based on his testimony alone," says Radakovich. "especially since I put Arroyo's wife on the stand to testify that he was home with her the whole time."

But he admits that, watching the jury, he grew worried.

As for the defendants, the whole procedure was a nightmare of mounting confusion. Their four separate lawyers had to use court-supplied translators. Though Radakovich speaks fluent Spanish, he was translating not only for his client but often for the extended families and friends of the defendants as well. According to Arroyo, the men on trial never fully understood what was happening. They couldn't understand why Joaquin's recanted statement was entered during their trial. They couldn't understand why their lawyers didn't refute it.

"It was a mess," Arroyo says.

There was no way that Radakovich could adequately convey to his client his greatest worry. He had a sinking feeling that whatever decision the jury reached, the judge would de-cide the same. "I just had this feeling that the judge, who's a fine judge, don't get me wrong, was letting himself be swayed by the evidence entered in the jury trial."

After eight days of testimony, the jury finally retired. "I urged the judge to write down his decision right then, while the jury was still out," Radakovich says. "He told me he didn't want there to be any possibility of his decision having influenced the jury. So I said, fine. Just write it down and seal it. He could open it after the jury came in. But he refused."

Judge Kenneth Gillis has a ready explanation: "My practice," he says, "was, where the jury was out, I would not rule until the jury came back with their decision. This was because I didn't want my verdict to influence the jury if they heard from court personnel or people around the courtroom what I'd decided." He says he doesn't recall any lawyers in the trial asking him to seal his decision.

The jury stayed out overnight. The next morning, it announced the verdict. The jurors found Joaquin guilty of four counts of murder, two counts of aggravated battery, and six counts of armed violence. Almost immediately, Judge Gillis announced his verdicts: He found Rogelio Arroyo, Isauro Sanchez, and Uncle Nacho guilty of the same charges. The mandatory sentence for anyone convicted of multiple murder in Illinois is natural life. No parole. No reduced sentence. You die in prison.

The men appealed. The Illinois Appellate Court upheld the trial court's conviction. The men did not attempt to bring their case before the Illinois Supreme Court.

The four sit today, as they have for the past eight years, in prison. The only hope they have now is a last-resort appeal under the Post-Conviction Act. One of its provisions allows for the consideration of new evidence. If it is significant enough, the judge who originally heard the case can call for a retrial.

There does seem to be new evidence in this case. After the men were sentenced, Uncle Nacho's brother sought out and found the four men who had fled to Mexico, and got them to write down their version of what happened that night. The four documents that resulted use very similar wording. Each says that the four men now serving time are "innocents of such case." The statements go on to say that the four men now in Mexico are "guilty of the murders." Each of these confessions is signed by one of the men. The documents are now in the possession of Gary Adair, the new attorney for all of the defendants except Isauro Sanchez. Adair is trying to establish their authenticity.

* * *

MATTER AS INDICATED:
TO CIVIL AND MILITARY AUTHORITIES
BY MEANS OF THIS LETTER I DECLARE THE FOLLOWING:

I GILBERTO VARELA FIGUEROA, AM RESPONSIBLE OF THE ACCIDENT OCCURRED ON NOVEMBER 26, 1981 AT 2121 N. MILWAUKEE, CHICAGO, ILLINOIS. SAUL VARELA MONTES DE OCA, IRINEO TRUJILLO ARROYO. WE ALL ARE GUILTY OF THE MURDERS OF ARNULFO SANCHEZ FIGUEROA, RAMON SANCHEZ FIGUEROA, ELIODORO SANCHEZ FIGUEROA, VALENTE GALINDO RAMIREZ. THEREFORE MR. IGNACIO VARELA FIGUEROA, JOAQUIN VARELA ARROYO, YSAGRO SANCHEZ VARELA AND ROGELIO ARROYO

ARE INOCENTS OF THIS CASE. THEY ARE INOCENTS OF SUCH CASE. MR. LIONSO QUEZADA LIED IN HIS DECLARATION. WE THE MENTIONED PEOPLE ARE THE MUDERERS. THIS IS ALL I HAVE TO SAY.

WITHOUT NOTHING FURTHER TO SAY, TRULY YOURS.
GILBERTO VARELA FIGUEROA

****

Even more compelling is the phone call Margo De Ley received from Gilberto Varela. "Ramiro, I, Saul and Irineo were there and did the shooting," he told her. He even provided a scorecard: he'd killed one Sanchez; Irineo had killed another; Ramiro had killed a third Sanchez and shot Leoncio Quezada; Saul shot Rogelio Medina and another man, Valente Galindo.

Would he be willing to make an official statement to that effect? De Ley asked him. Yes, he said. If one were sent to him in Mexico, he'd sign and return it. Would he also be willing to return to Chicago, where a fugitive warrant has been issued for him and speak on behalf of his imprisoned relatives?

"Sure," he said, suddenly sounding resigned. "Why not?"

He promised to call De Ley back, but hasn't. Other people confirm the caller's version of events. One is Francelia Varela, the 22-year-old daughter of Uncle Nacho and niece of the fugitive Ramiro. Now living in Bucktown, she's one of the few residents of that neighborhood willing to be quoted. "I'm not afraid of anybody," she says.

In 1982, just after the murders, she was in Guerrero with her family, waiting for word about her father. Suddenly, in

February of that year, Ramiro Varela arrived and seemed unable to stop talking about the murders. Look, here's what happened, he told them. We had no choice because they had knives. I told them to calm down but one of them called me a pinche rengo (fucking asshole) and threatened me with a knife, so I shot him.

Francelia says they were all stunned when they got word that her father had been convicted. "Ramiro told us not to worry. Don't cry, he said. Your father is innocent and he doesn't owe anything. They'll all get out because they didn't do anything."

Ramiro stayed in Guerrero for a few months, then left. Francelia has no idea where he is today.

After eight years, one actual eyewitness to the murders has come forth. Rodolfo Carreon is serving a life sentence for an unrelated murder. He doesn't worry anymore about deportation, so he's willing to talk. At the time of the murders he owned a barbershop across the street from 2121 North Milwaukee. He was there late that night, when a bullet whizzed through the window.

"I saw someone running across the street and down Milwaukee, and behind him was another man, shooting at him. I saw his face well. Also there was another man who stopped in the street, took his pistol in both hands to aim, and shot at someone."

Carreon is in the same prison with the men and says he is absolutely certain none of them were the shooters he saw that night.

Told of this, Radakovich says, "Damn. I wish we'd had that eight years ago. I hope to God it does some good. I really think Arroyo, and probably the other guys, too, got shafted."

Gary Adair, the men's new attorney, is hopeful but not altogether sure of the chances for a new trial. The new evidence is suggestive, he says, and it is compelling. But he needs far more—more eyewitnesses, more detailed statements from the men in Mexico, more proof —if he's to win a reversal.

Margo De Ley, who has been completely caught up in the men's story, is still running down leads. She is trying to find other eyewitnesses and persuade them to come forward. She's talked to people at the Mexican Consulate. The Mexican Ministry of Foreign Affairs in Mexico City is watching the developments in the case.

"I just believe so strongly about this whole case," De Ley says. "I went to the prisons and met the men. And I was more convinced than ever that they've been wronged."

Postscript

This story appeared in Chicago Magazine, in May 1990, and shortly thereafter Governor James Thompson of Illinois ordered an investigation into the case. In January 1991 Thompson commuted the sentences of all four men to time served. He left it up to his successor, Jim Edgar, whether they should receive a full pardon. In September 1991 Edgar pardoned them.

Danny's Boat

Danny's Boat

There are several references within this story to a snapshot of four young men standing on the deck of a boat rigged for sailing. The photo appeared with the story when it was first published, in 1986. It went missing in 2002, after it was used in the production of an anthology, so it does not appear here. That's no great loss graphically. What makes the photo interesting is the fact that two of those men murdered the other two less than an hour after it was taken.

The killers are Frenchmen, names unknown, referred to in the story as "the Corsican-looking one" and his "putty-nosed pal." The victims are Danny Seymour, whom the story concerns, and Bob Breckenridge, an American Danny hired on as a crewman in Cartagena, Colombia. Danny and Bob don't know they're going to die, but the Frenchmen know they are going to kill them. The temptation was to read all that into their expressions, but I never could.

Danny Seymour posed a conundrum for anyone who wanted to give him a gift on his 27th birthday. He'd never lacked for material things, and claimed he had way more than he wanted. On top of that he was talented, he knew lots of interesting people, two good women loved him, and the cream of the 1970s underground frequented his Bowery loft. You might say he had it all. Nevertheless, he told friends who had gathered for a party that he was practically in a state of despair.

"Nothing can change for me until my money is gone," he declared. "I want to be broke."

That was Danny at his worst, the poor little rich kid whining about his fate. Snap out of it! more than one of his guests wanted to tell him, but they knew that he'd probably redeem himself with an act of generosity, an insight distilled from his extraordinary life, or just his flair for having a good time and making sure everyone else did too. Before the evening was over, Danny had shown some photos he had taken during the Paris uprising of May '68. He'd held the phone out so his friends could hear Keith Richards sing him "Happy Birthday" from London. He'd passed around a signed first edition of Old Possum's Book of Practical Cats by T. S. Eliot, and described how it had been presented to him by his mother, the poet Isabella Gardner, in a fit of alcohol-induced largesse. She'd attempted to retrieve the book many times, offering money or items of value in return, because she'd decided he lacked the refinement to appreciate it. "No thanks," Danny would reply, we're using it to prop a window open."

A few weeks after that party, Danny plunked down $70,000 cash for a thirty-eight-foot wooden yacht, sailed away, and—in April 1973—just disappeared.

Rumors soon began to surface among his friends. He had been hijacked and murdered by pirates. He was living as an anonymous beach bum on the San Blas Islands. The CIA had killed him. The CIA had saved him. Likewise the Mafia, or a cabal made up of both organizations because their disparate agendas just happened to concur in respect to Danny.

In other words, he was doing what he always did, living out other people's fantasies.

Danny came from one of America's oldest and wealthiest families, the Gardners of Boston. His mother, niece and namesake of the art collector Isabella Stewart Gardner, traced her ancestry to Mary Queen of Scots. She'd studied drama in England and acted on the London stage from 1939 to the outbreak of World War II. Then she returned to the United States and began writing poetry seriously, a decision that served as an inspiration to her cousin, Robert Lowell. They both became major poets, while their more practical kinsmen got on with the family business, investment banking for the men, marrying well for the women.

Isabella didn't always marry well, but she married often. Her second husband, Maurice Seymour, a Russian Jewish show business photographer, was Danny's father. They lived in Chicago, where Isabella joined the staff of Poetry Magazine. One of her duties was to use her name and connections to acquire funding. That was how she met her third husband (one of her better marriages), the developer and real estate tycoon, Robert H. McCormick Jr.

By age seven Danny was living in a home in which architects Mies Van der Rohe and Walter Gropius, plus every literary light that lived in or passed through Chicago—Karl Shapiro, Dylan Thomas, Reuel Denney, and Galway Kinnell, to name just a few—showed up for drinks. Young Danny, who had been given a camera by his father, began taking their pictures. He had found his vocation.

Later he would gain a reputation in Minneapolis based on his whimsical half-photo, half-drawings, but that phase didn't last long. He soon abandoned original work in favor of what he knew best, photographs of the famous people he rubbed shoulders with. A book of Danny's photos titled A Loud Song was published by Listrum Press in 1971. Ted Hartwell, former curator of photography at the Minneapolis Institute of Arts, who organized a show of Danny's work in 1967, put his finger on the nature of his gift.

"Some of his photos were excellent," said Hartwell, "but he won't be remembered so much for their quality as for his amazing knack for being in the midst of interesting people and situations, and capturing them on film."

Danny's interesting life did not include much fathering after his mother divorced Maurice Seymour. Isabella's younger brother, George Peabody Gardner Jr., tried to take up the slack for a few years. George, an amateur archaeologist, showed Danny how to search for artifacts during summer hikes on Cape Cod. He taught him how to fish for trout in a stream near the family's Wellfleet estate, and how to sail, first on Wellfleet Bay, then off a nearby point where the seas could be treacherous. He had plenty of time to spend with Danny. After graduating from Harvard and rising to the rank of lieutenant commander in the Navy, he took a decade off. Besides tutoring his nephew in what Danny's grandfather, George Gardner Sr., dubbed "the fine art of fucking around," he went mountain climbing, spent a year in Mexico digging in the Mayan ruins, dabbled in journalism, became a regular at east coast sailing regattas, and married a Russian ballerina after a stormy courtship.

Gardner made an excellent companion for a young boy, but in the end he proved to be a man of predictable interests, and Danny wasn't one of them. His transformation from surrogate dad to disapproving uncle coincided with the blossoming of his own financial career. In 1955 he became a partner at the investment banking firm of Paine, Webber, Jackson and Curtis, and shortly thereafter his father arranged a seat for him on the board of United Fruit, a company in which the family was a major holder.

George Gardner was well qualified for the post, not only by background, but because of his Navy contacts. United Fruit had been the dominant power in the Caribbean basin for more than fifty years, but the company was being tested by local insurgencies and had become increasingly reliant on its ties with the armed forces and the intelligence community.

Danny asked his mother if he could drop out of prep school and come home when he was sixteen. You're too young, she replied. A year later he asked again. You're too old, she told him. By then she was living in Minneapolis with her fourth husband, the critic and poet Alan Tate, who taught at the University of Minnesota.

Danny came to Minneapolis anyway. He rented an apartment not far from his mother's home, set up a tiny darkroom in the basement, and began making a life for himself. His place soon became the headquarters for a bunch of young photographers, two of whom, Paco Grande and Steven Arhelger, were his lifelong friends.

Days and nights at Danny's flowed seamlessly into one long party, and the line between work and play blurred. Danny happened on one of the more startling effects in his repertoire when he lit a joint in the darkroom, and created a flare of exposure across a face floating in a tray of developer. He and Grande used red wine for toner in a series of maroon nudes. Grande introduced Danny to his first serious girlfriend, Phyllis Cooney.

"I inherit half a million dollars when I'm 21," he once complained to Cooney. "Have you ever tried to ignore something like that?"

"Not until I met you," she replied.

Danny's ambivalence about his wealth did not go unnoticed. "He'd be in a room full of people trying to be one of the crowd," says his friend Steve Kaplan, "but it was always clear to him that the minute he left someone would say, 'Know who that was? Danny Seymour the millionaire.'"

In the 1960s, Kaplan, Danny, and writer Billy Golfus published a magazine called In Beat, which chronicled the Twin Cities music scene. It featured interviews with big names like Bob Dylan along with local bands—The Trashmen, The Castaways—and opined on some of the day's burning questions, i.e., "Is Mod out?"

There was a purposeful effort not to let the war in Vietnam spoil the fun at In Beat, but the big issues affected Danny deeply. "He was as anti-war as anybody," said his friend Steve Arhelger, "but he took the stuff about corporate war criminals personally. It just tore him up. His attitude toward his uncle George was all over the place. He loved him, he felt abandoned by him, he despised United Fruit and everything it stood for; he thought the Gardner money was dirty, but he wanted it anyway. People dismissed Danny's problems because he was rich, but he was in pain."

Which may explain another aspect of his character. "He was always excessive," Kaplan says, "and he fancied excess, if you know what I mean. That was his self-image, the excessive, burn-out artist. He talked a lot about early death."

He got his wish in that regard, but he never did shrug off the yoke of privilege. The Gardner family's power and influence would provide an intriguing epilogue to Danny's short, strange life.

****

Danny's uncle, George Gardner Jr., stood squarely in the tradition of the filibusteros, a Spanish term for predatory adventurer, coined to describe the Americans who came to the Caribbean basin to exploit its resources. The archetype filibustero was Minor Keith, a ruthless Yankee engineer possessed of an odd capitalist genius that didn't kick in until his back was to the wall. The president of Costa Rica hired Keith to build a railroad from that country's coffee-producing highlands to the coast in 1872.

More than a thousand of Keith's workers died during the first two years of construction, amid conditions so gruesome that he couldn't recruit new laborers. He was down to a skeleton crew and progress was measured in inches per day when he made a deal with the Louisiana prison system to send him 700 inmates to toil in the jungle. All but 25 of them died of backbreaking work and tropical diseases before construction ended in 1890.

Thus was a great enterprise born in blood and travail, but it wasn't the Costa Rican railroad.

Keith's project had been plagued by financial crises, resulting in the chronic threat of starvation for his workers. Desperate, he hit on the idea of planting banana trees along the route to feed them, which ultimately led to the formation of a profitable company that transported bananas to the coast via railroad, and exported them to the USA.

In 1899, financial problems again forced Keith's hand. He traveled to Boston to make a deal with his main rival,

Andrew Preston, president of the Boston Fruit Company. The two merged interests, forming the United Fruit Company on March 30, 1899.

That same year the first boatload of bananas left the republic of Honduras, bound for New Orleans. The boat and its cargo belonged to the Cuyamel Fruit Company, owned by Samuel ("Sam the Banana Man") Zemurray.

In 1929, after an unsuccessful price war against Zemurray, United Fruit merged with its rival. The Banana Man became the biggest shareholder in United Fruit. When he retired as president of the company in 1951, Zemurray was the only power that mattered in Central America. He meddled unabashedly in the region's politics, using bribery, intimidation and mercenary goon squads to get his way. His base of operations, Honduras, always the quintessential banana republic, remains the region's most reliable U.S. ally. It has served as the staging ground for many U.S. intelligence operations, including the shadow war against the Nicaraguan Sandinistas in the 1980s, and the coup in 1954 against Jacobo Arbenz, president of Guatemala, a democratically elected leftist who made no secret of his desire to throw United Fruit out of his country.

Among the idealistic young Latin Americans who flocked to Guatemala to fight "The Octopus" (their term for United Fruit) was an Argentinean named Ernesto "Che" Guevara. He fled just ahead of the coup and took refuge in Mexico City. There he hooked up with Fidel Castro, who was planning a revolution in his home country of Cuba.

Cuba's proximity to the United States made it ground zero for filibusteros from the late nineteenth century on, a tradition that flowered spectacularly in the 1950s when American mobsters acquired the major hotel and casino operations in Havana. Meyer Lansky operated the Montmartre and the Havana Hilton. Santo Trafficante Jr. grabbed the Capri. American Gangsters turned whoring and gambling into industries in Cuba.

Marquee wise guys were just the whitecap on a wave of hoods who hung out in Havana in the 1950s. "You walk into one of these Cuban gambling joints," reported Newsweek in 1954, "it's like walking on to the set of a Grade-B gangster movie." The similarity was particularly uncanny at the Capri, where George Raft, who played so many gangsters he began to think he was one, welcomed guests with his patented Scarface snarl.

Another multiple personality was a frequent visitor to Havana, a Chicagoan named Richard Cain who sometimes took on other personas, including that of a Mafioso called Ricardo Scalzetti. Cain flew there whenever he could get time off from his job as a detective on the Chicago police force. A handsome, glib, tough guy who spoke five languages, Cain was making a career out of playing both ends against the middle. His knowledge of mob activities had already proven invaluable to the Chicago police, and by the mid-1950s he had shown the mob that the information he could provide about the police was just as useful to them. Even at that early stage of his decades-long career both law enforcement and the mob humored Cain's eccentricities, calling him by any name he chose to use, because his skills and the bold way he used them made him uniquely valuable.

Havana in the 1950s was a fantasy of exotic music, erotic stage shows and the rush of high-stakes gambling, but when Fidel Castro rode into town on a tank in 1959 the dream was over. The gangsters tried to do business with Castro, but he refused.

The loss of their Cuban fiefdom enraged the mob, and they plotted with the CIA to assassinate him. Most historians believe that Santo Trafficante and Chicagoan Johnny Rosselli, who were jointly in charge of the contract on Castro's life, quickly saw the folly of the project and simply fed the CIA tall tales of near misses in return for the agency's money. If any credible attempt was made, Richard Cain was the man who made it, according to the report of a U.S. Senate committee that investigated the CIA in the 1970s.

"Cain was connected to La Cosa Nostra, spoke fluent Spanish, and had extensive contacts in Latin America," according to the committee's report. It concluded that Cain had been on Chicago mobster Salvatore "Momo" Giancana's payroll since 1956, and in 1960 tried to arrange Castro's assassination at his behest. A Cuban hooker of Cain's acquaintance was supposed to seduce Castro and poison his drink. It almost worked.

Mobsters were not the only ones who took Castro's revolution personally. Danny's uncle George had become chairman of the United Fruit board and president of the company shortly after the Arbenz coup in Guatemala. He was considered the kind of bright, well-connected young executive who could clean up the company's tarnished image and boost its profitability. He viewed United Fruit's Cuban sugar mills as the key to increasing revenues. Castro's decision to nationalize them stuck in his craw.

It is a matter of record that the Cuban refugee force that engaged Castro's army at the Bay of Pigs made liberal use of United Fruit's resources, especially its communications facilities on an island off the coast of Honduras. Rumors about the company's role in the plots to assassinate Castro were rampant but never substantiated.

* * *

In 1967, as Danny's 21st birthday approached, he began laying plans to leave Minneapolis and begin spending his inheritance. By then he and Paco Grande were hanging around the University of Minnesota's studio arts department, where another friend, Jay Hines, taught photography. The buzz around the darkroom concerned an adventure that was brewing. Danny was going to take Grande, Hines, and whoever else struck his fancy, to Europe to make films. About a week before departure Hines introduced Danny to one of his students, a girl named Jessica Lange, who quickly became part of the retinue. She and Grande later married.

When Danny and his twelve-person entourage hit Paris, the 1968 uprising was in full swing, but he took only a few shots of the action. He opted instead for pictures of the personalities he encountered in a café on Rue D'Bac, the center of a scene that included British pop stars and political heavies who spent their days on the ramparts, like Danny the Red. Rolling Stones guitarist Keith Richards and his bodyguard Tom Keylock swept through frequently as well. Richards and Danny began a friendship that they would renew a few years later in the United States.

Lange and Grande stuck with Danny after everyone else left for home. The three of them flew to New York City and took up residence in 1969. Danny moved into a loft on the Bowery with his new girlfriend, a dancer from California named Kate Moore.

Danny and Kate's loft became a rendezvous for photographers. A school of photography evolved there, a kind of documentary surrealism. Photographers Danny Lyons and Larry Clark are associated with that style, along with Danny. All three reflect the influence of Robert Frank, who lived one floor below. Danny fronted the money for Clark's book Tulsa, which has become a collector's item.

It was possible to run into anyone from pop stars to buskers at Danny's loft, but the person an occasional guest was most likely to run into was Ernie Holman, a bodyguard-sized black man who was bouncer and part owner of the Five Spot, a lower East Side jazz lounge. Holman was found shot to death in his apartment a year after Danny disappeared. Some of Danny's friends were convinced that their deaths were related, but no connection ever surfaced, other than the obvious one. They both used heroin. Drugs had begun to play a central role in Danny's life after he moved to New York, and it became an issue in his relationship with Moore.

In December 1970, Yoko Ono was looking for a place to shoot her film, titled Fly. She decided to use Danny's loft, and Danny took the opportunity to make a movie about her and John Lennon.

It opened with Danny's signature shot, an overexposed blur that gradually darkened and focused to reveal an image. It was Lennon, sitting on the couch playing a tune that he was creating on the spot. Then an outtake from Ono's film appeared, a fly seen through a magnifying lens, picking its way through a tangled mass of pubic hair.

Danny's film showed Ono auditioning dozens of naked actresses in search of the right backdrop for The Fly, a process that involved pointing a light meter at the crucial portion of anatomy, and shouting out readings. Lennon stayed off to the side and cracked jokes in a cockney accent.

It was Danny's best cinematic effort, a portrait of two of the essential figures of an era just as their era was coming to a close. He and Ono discussed a possible collaboration during the filming, but Danny wasn't much interested. He had his eye on a boat, he told her. He wanted to sail away for a time, to clean up. Moore agreed to accompany him, but only if kicking heroin was truly the agenda.

Before they could leave, Danny lucked into one more adventure. His friend Robert Frank had done the cover art for the Rolling Stones album Exile on Main Street. The Stones liked his work, and invited Frank to chronicle their 1972 tour of the United States on film. Frank asked Danny to come along as cameraman.

The Stones were at the height of their fame. They were whisked from city to city in a private jet, grabbing whoever amused them and taking them along. Frank wanted to film things as they were, and they were pretty earthy. The movie that resulted, Cocksucker Blues, is under permanent injunction by the Stones limiting it to one private showing per year. Frank has referred to it as a portrait of three people: Mick Jagger, Keith Richards, and Danny Seymour. If so, it makes a fitting epitaph for Danny and his times. They were gaudy and self-indulgent, easy to find fault with but interesting in ways that have rarely been duplicated since.

A few months after the tour ended, rumors began making their way to Minneapolis. Danny was lost at sea. Piracy was suspected. His disappearance was part of some larger plot. The CIA was involved, or the Mafia, or both. It sounded like the kind of drama Danny might have scripted for his curtain call.

Danny had named his boat the Immamou, after a Haitian deity, and set sail from Miami in October 1972. Aboard were Moore, her two-year-old son, Jason, and two friends, Susan and Robert Duran. They were bound for Jamaica, Haiti, and South America.

The voyage began idyllically, with frequent stops on beautiful, isolated little islands, but Moore felt duped by the caches of drugs that kept turning up aboard ship, and caring for a two-year-old at sea was a full-time task. By the time they reached Haiti in March 1973, the Durans were tired of Kate and Danny's quarrels, and they returned to the United States. Moore decided to stick with Danny for the time being despite the drugs. They set sail from Port au Prince, bound for Cartagena, Colombia.

It was a hellish trip. Foul, dangerous weather plagued them to within a few miles of the South American coast. There the clouds lifted, and gentle northeast breezes, the fabled "trade winds" of the Caribbean, ushered them into port. But at the height of the gale, a day out of Port au Prince, they had to lash Jason into his bunk so they'd have one less potential disaster on their hands. Jason's terrified cries were so loud that they rose above the wailing wind, but Moore couldn't go below and comfort him. When the storm was finally over there were still twenty-foot swells and intermittent squalls to contend with. There was no way one person could handle the boat for long. At best one of them could crash for an hour, while the other held the rudder with one hand and controlled the main spar by rope with the other. That was the drill, day and night. The compass spun wildly, the radio went dead, they were blown off course many times, but Danny always managed to get them pointed in the right direction again. By the

time they made port, they were sleep deprived and emotionally exhausted.

Shortly after they docked, Moore told Danny she wanted
out. I guess I can't blame you, Danny said. He was exhausted
too, but Moore's decision put him in a bind. As their recent
voyage had demonstrated, it took a minimum of three capable
hands to sail the Immamou, preferably four, and now he was
down to one.

There wasn't a seat to be had on a Miami-bound plane
for a week, so Kate and Danny had to keep on going through
the motions. It was excruciating, Moore recalls, an emotional
ordeal tacked on to the physical one they'd just been through.
There wasn't much to do but wander around the docks, and on
one of those strolls they met Bob Breckenridge, an American
kid who called himself a boat-watcher, meaning he stayed
aboard rich people's vessels while they took side trips.

Breckenridge was a few years younger than Danny and
Moore. He had dropped out of college to see the world,
and ended up in Cartagena for the same reason most people
did—cocaine.

In the early 1970s, when the Colombian cocaine industry
was still taking shape and smuggling routes had yet to be es-
tablished, Cartagena bulged at the seams with cocaine, most
of it in the form of basuco, a raw, crack-like preparation.
For a brief moment in history, supply outstripped demand.
Throwaway kids who slept in doorways laced their mooched
cigarettes with basuco. Warehouses full of basuco sat waiting for a buyer—any buyer. Macho outlaws, among them an
enterprising car thief named Pablo Escobar, took advantage
of standing offers of one million dollars cash to fly plane
loads of refined product into the United States. Anyone with

a boat could fill the hold with cheap cocaine and take a stab at getting rich.

For most aspiring smugglers, obtaining the boat was a bigger problem than acquiring the payload, an imperative that drove the long tradition of Caribbean piracy to a new stage. Pirates no longer attacked boats to steal cargo. They hijacked boats to smuggle cargo, and rarely left any witnesses to tell the tale. The boats were generally sunk after one or two runs.

In 1975, a U.S. House subcommittee chaired by Representative John Murphy of New York heard evidence that more than 600 U.S. registered pleasure craft and two thousand of their crew members had disappeared during the period 1971-74. A witness testified that bad weather and bad luck might account for twenty missing boats. The rest, the committee concluded, fell prey to narco-piracy.

Danny may have heard of the danger, but he had few options. He could abandon his boat and the way of life it represented, or he could find a crew. Breckenridge told him he was more than willing to help sail the boat, whatever the destination, and he knew of two experienced sailors who might feel the same. Moore remembers him saying they were French.

The Frenchmen's names have been blacked out of the files on the matter of "Daniel Seymour and Robert Kent Breckenridge - Crime on the High Seas." Moore recalls Danny referring to them as "the two Rs," which sounds like him (he used to tell friends that his five-star prep school education had succeeded in imparting less than two of the three Rs). Raoul and Robert? Ricard and Roland? Moore can't remember. At the time she couldn't have cared less. She was busy preparing for her departure, which finally took place on April 25, 1973. She and Danny arranged to meet in Miami a few months later to discuss their relationship. Meanwhile Moore and her son flew to her hometown of San Francisco.

On May 19, someone from a yacht named the Chesapeake asked Danny, Bob Breckenridge and the two Rs to pose for a picture. They were busy preparing to sail, but took time to gather on deck for the photo. Later that day Danny signed out of the Port of Cartagena, bound for Colon, Panama, a voyage that takes three days with a following wind, up to a week if extensive tacking is required.

Danny had promised to call Moore from Panama as soon as he docked, but weeks passed, then a month, with no word. Moore kept her worries to herself as long as she could and then called Danny's mother, who contacted her brother George.

George Gardner began pulling strings. Soon the US. Navy, the Coast Guard, the DEA, the FBI, and several branches of US. Intelligence were in the midst of a highly unusual search for a private citizen's vessel outside the territorial waters of the United States. A letter from Gardner in the FBI file, dated July 24, 1973, describes the Immamou, takes note of "the problems of jurisdiction and other problems as well," and thanks Navy Commander M. K. Phillips for the efforts he has already made.

How extraordinary were those efforts? According to the House committee that investigated boat disappearances, they were unprecedented. The committee concluded that the DEA, the Coast Guard, and the FBI, each of which had legitimate grounds for investigating the rash of hijackings, routinely ignored the phenomenon.

The Coast Guard had taken note of the disappearances as early as spring 1971, but inexplicably sat on a warning it intended to issue until a committee investigator prodded them on the matter years later. The DEA was concentrating on buy-and-bust tactics targeting low-level dealers in order to build statistics, and feared taking on a problem as intractable as narco-piracy. Nonetheless, both agencies joined what amounted to an official government search for Danny's boat. By August 1973, the Caribbean was being systematically combed for the Immamou.

Late that month, Moore received a letter from a kindred soul she and Danny had met in Jamaica, a hippy named Rico. He and his girlfriend Sarah were still sailing the Caribbean on their ship the Pogo.

The letter, postmarked August 23 from Cartagena, began: "I have heard some rather strange stories since arriving here about Danny and crew. I hope everything is as it should be, but if not I should tell you what I know." Rico explained that he had seen the Immamou a few weeks after Danny sailed from Cartagena. It was docked at Port Royal, Jamaica, with only the Frenchmen aboard.

"The big fancy yacht Chesapeake was in Port Royal at the time," he writes. "They knew Danny from Cartagena, and talked to the French fellows about him. They got the story that Danny was strung out on coke and had split when they reached the San Blas Islands, planning to fly to New York. But funny thing, when I tried to talk to them about it they claimed to speak no English (one didn't speak very well, but the other spoke perfect English I later learned). All very strange. Another fellow left Cartagena with them, he hasn't been seen either, I understand you haven't heard from Danny, and I'm told people have come here looking for him."

Along with the letter, Rico enclosed the picture taken from the Chesapeake, somewhat the worse for wear but clearly showing Danny, Breckenridge, and the two Frenchmen on the deck of the Immamou shortly before they sailed.

The news froze Moore. She knew that Danny's uncle should have the information, but her contact with him was through Isabella Gardner. Isabella had divorced Alan Tate. She was living alone in Los Angeles, and in fragile shape. More bad news might be the death of her, Moore reasoned, yet George Gardner had to be informed.

Besides worrying about Danny and his mother, Moore had problems of her own. Earning money was something she hadn't thought about for a long time. She had left Cartagena with enough to get by until she and Danny met in Miami. Now she was beginning to wonder whether she would ever see Danny again, but doing anything practical to improve her situation seemed like giving up on him.

One evening, while she was sitting around pondering her predicament, a man named Mr. Brown knocked on her door and solved all her problems.

Brown, a dapper, fiftyish fellow, said he was a detective looking for Danny. "He told me something that I guess sounded a little strange," she recalls, years after the fact. "He didn't say George Gardner had hired him. He said he owed George a favor, and that was why he was trying to find Danny."

But that discordant note was lost in a veritable symphony of upbeat talk. Brown was optimistic about locating Danny, and indicated that he might be able to help Moore too. He was a perfect gentleman, but with just enough flirt in his demeanor to charm a young woman. He told Moore that if she used his name, an associate of his who owned a nightclub in the Bay Area would hire her. He inquired if she had any information that might be useful in his search for Danny. She handed over

Rico's letter and the picture, but only after he promised they would be returned.

Brown kissed her hand by way of farewell and said something in French. She remembers feeling better after his visit than she had felt in a long time.

Brown was as good as his word. The letter and the picture showed up in her mailbox about a week later. By then she had inquired about the nightclub job. It turned out to be a topless joint, and the owner gave her the creeps. She didn't take the job, but just checking it out got her going again, and she soon found work more to her liking. She never articulated it, not even to herself, but Brown's visit had prompted her to accept her loss and move on.

Two copies of the picture were sent to Commander M. K. Phillips, U.S. Navy, along with a letter, author's name deleted (one of hundreds of deletions in FBI file 45-11278, most of them accompanied by the explanation that they would "disclose the identity of an individual or an agency conducting a lawful national intelligence operation"). According to the letter, "Dan Seymour is on the left with the hat and the cigarette, and Breckenridge is on the right." Whatever it says about the Frenchmen (almost ten lines' worth) is deleted. Their figures are blacked out in the reproduction of the photograph contained in the file.

On November 27, 1973, about six weeks after Brown visited Moore, the Coast Guard received a tip, which was passed on to several other agencies, including the FBI. The supplier of the tip is identified as "special agent (deleted)." The author of the memo writes that "(deleted) is a pseudonym." The tip comes in the form of a brief message written in French and partially translated as, "It seems odd to me that 'coast watchers' at St. Bart's would be able to dig up info unobtainable by your guys. I understand the problems though, and am grateful for your help."

The rest of the message is deleted, but it must have specified the Immamou's location. Of the 183 American pleasure craft listed as missing in winter 1972-73, the Immamou was the only one ever located. It was spotted in the open sea shortly after the tip was received, and tailed thereafter by a motorized boat.

* * *

After they came under surveillance, the Frenchmen altered course and headed straight for the French island of Guadeloupe, a good jurisdiction from their perspective. In early December they docked at Pointe-a-Pitre, where they were immediately arrested by French authorities. The Immamou was impounded.

The files only hint at the sequence of events leading to their capture, but it is reasonable to infer that Brown started tracing Danny's boat from Port Royal on the basis of the letter Moore gave him. Either Brown or someone connected with him is the "coast watcher" who spotted the Immamou. Brown is the author of the tip.

"A lawyer has been down to Guadeloupe and what he reports is quite terrifying," Isabella Gardner wrote Moore, in December 1973. "He discovered that 2 yachts and several individuals had previously disappeared as a result of the Frenchmen's machinations."

In another letter, Danny's mother reports that the Frenchmen are out of jail, but must stay in Guadeloupe until a civil action concerning the ownership of the Immamou is settled.

"The French are notorious for cruelty in getting prisoners to talk," she writes. "God knows why the Frenchmen did not tell something about Daniel and Keith B. Oh God, where is he?"

Of course, she knew where he was, and how he got there. The lawyer she refers to in her letter had discovered even more than she conveyed to Moore. Colombian authorities were certain that the Frenchmen had been involved in five murders. The lack of a corpse had precluded prosecution in Colombia. It would ultimately have the same result in Guadeloupe.

Throughout the month that they'd languished in the Pointe-a-Pitre lockup, the Frenchmen stuck to their story. Then they continued to stick to it throughout their 14 month confinement on the island: They had been invited aboard the Immamou by its owner, Danny Seymour. He had turned his boat over to them when he and Breckenridge went ashore on one of the San Blas Islands. Both Americans were too strung out on drugs to remain at sea. They had all planned to meet in Miami in March 1974, where Danny would again take possession of his boat.

Their tale reeked of expedience, but it was impossible to disprove. Three bullet holes were discovered in the Immamou's saloon. The Frenchmen pleaded ignorance. Queried whether they wanted to assert ownership of Danny's boat, they answered no. Had they said yes they would have been charged with piracy, but they knew better.

That was how things stood in January 1974 when Moore was thumbing through Time magazine one day, and was startled to see Mr. Brown's picture under the headline "Double-Dealer's Death." The story concerned the assassination of well-known gangster Richard Cain, who had been murdered on Chicago's "hairy, scary west side." He had been killed just a short time after he located Danny's boat.

"I was really frightened," Moore says, and her fears were not soothed by the advice she received in a letter from Isabella Gardner. "For some reason my brother wants to keep both you and me out of all this. SAY NOTHING TO THE FBI OR ANYONE."

According to the Time magazine story, "On the afternoon of December 21st, 1973, two armed men wearing ski masks walked into a sandwich shop where Cain was drinking coffee, and ordered everybody in the place up against the wall. One of the gunmen then shoved a shotgun under the chin of Cain, 49. The hit man fired two blasts, blowing away Cain's handsome face."

Witnesses said the killers were accompanied when they fled by a mysterious woman Cain had been talking with before he was murdered. "Thus ended Cain's remarkable, double-dealing life as a policeman and a mobster," said the article.

The question the story raised but failed to answer was, who killed Cain and why? In death as in life, Cain was an enigma. A Chicago gossip columnist had once described him as, "a compulsive adventurer who wasn't happy unless his life was in danger."

A relentless publicity hound, Cain often claimed that his real name was Ricardo Scalzetti, and that he had been born and raised in Chicago's First Ward, just a few blocks from where he was gunned down. Not so, according to the Chicago Tribune (in its front-page coverage of the assassination): "An investigator who made an extensive inquiry into his life, said his name really was Cain, and his father came from a family that farmed near Owosso, Mich."

According to the investigator, Cain left high school at 17 and joined the army during World War II, using a forged birth certificate. Later he would regale gossip columnists with tales of his exploits in the Chinese underground, but he actually served as a company clerk in the Virgin Islands, where he learned to speak and write Spanish fluently. He worked as a private detective in Dallas and Miami after he was discharged, and developed an extensive network of contacts in both cities' law enforcement communities.

According to a memoir by his brother, Cain worked for a detective agency in Miami headed by a Cuban national named Guillermo Buenz. The agency had many clients in Cuba, among them higher-ups in the Batista regime, which was ousted by Castro. Cain reportedly met Chicago mobster Sam Giancana in 1950, while he was on assignment from Buenz in Havana.

In 1951, Cain went to a polygraph school in Chicago and joined the police force there a year later. In February 1959 he made headlines twice in Chicago.

The first came when Cain and his partner raided a prostitute's apartment and claimed they had seized $60,000 in cash, which they turned over as evidence. There was a scandal when the prostitute swore that $90,000 had been seized. Soon after that Cain was caught bugging the office of Mayor Richard Daley's organized crime task force, and placed on administrative leave. He immediately went to work for the Cook County state's attorney, and made headlines again when he killed a well-known gangster in a gunfight in downtown Chicago. It was ballyhooed as a brave act by a tough cop, but it would later be revealed as a hit contracted by rival gangsters.

Cain spent the next few years in Mexico, where he worked for the CIA and the State Department. He described his job as "tracing the flow of money into the hands of Central American revolutionaries." He also helped train anti-Castro Cubans for the Bay of Pigs invasion. It was during this period that he masterminded several unsuccessful attempts on Castro's life, according to the House Select Committee on Assassinations.

In his memoir, Cain's brother traces the line of authority for those attempts back to Robert Mahue, a former FBI man who specialized in arranging contacts between the CIA and U.S. business interests. Mahue's principal client was Howard Hughes. His main mob connection was Johnny Rosselli, who answered to Sam Giancana.

In 1962, Cain returned to Chicago, and went to work as chief investigator for the Cook County sheriff's office. He was still working for the sheriff in 1966 when the feds indicted him under the name Rico Scalzetti for his role in a 1963 bank robbery. He ultimately served three years in prison, a concurrent sentence for that crime and another robbery committed while he was working for the sheriff.

When he was released from prison in 1971, Cain publicly assumed a role that he had been playing covertly for years. He became Giancana's chief bodyguard and financial adviser. He had always been a prominent figure in Chicago's nightlife, but soon after his release sightings of him in the city's clubs became much less frequent. He and Giancana were spending most of their time in a heavily guarded fortress in Cuernavaca, Mexico, dodging subpoenas from government committees that were investigating the plots to kill Castro.

Cain had a chameleon-like gift for learning languages and taking on identities to go with them. He operated under many pseudonyms throughout his career as a double and triple agent. According to his putative boss, Giancana, he was up to his neck in the plot to assassinate John F. Kennedy. According to General Fabian Escalante Font, head of Cuban counterintelligence from 1976 to 1982, his investigators had concluded that Cain was a central figure in Kennedy's assassination.

An anonymous police investigator told Time magazine that Cain was killed "because he knew too much." He doesn't say what he knew, or why it might have marked him for death.

According to accounts of the murder in the Chicago papers, Cain entered Rose's Sandwich Shop about half an hour before he was killed, sat down at a table, and talked to four unidentified men, one of whom had a very dark suntan. The four men left, and minutes later an attractive woman, mid-thirties, olive skin, dark hair, dressed in black, joined Cain at his table.

Cain and the woman were talking when two men wearing ski masks came through the door, one toting a shotgun, the other holding a two-way radio in one hand and a pistol in the other. They ordered everybody in the place up against the wall—eight people including the proprietor, the waitress, the woman in black, Cain, and four customers.

The masked man with the radio conferred in hushed tones with someone outside. One of the customers heard a distinct "all clear," and then the masked man with the shotgun put the weapon under Cain's chin and shot him. When the smoke cleared, the other masked man reached into Cain's pants pocket and took something out. A voice over the radio inquired, "How does it look?" "OK," was the reply. "Then come on," the voice commanded. The gunmen left, accompanied by the woman in black.

Two days after the murder, an article appeared in the Chicago Tribune under the headline "Cain Was Informer, Federal Aides Reveal." It began by theorizing that Cain may have been killed when underworld leaders learned he was a government informant.

"Federal authorities said privately that Cain had provided them with information on and off for years and met with them regularly," said the article. "As recently as a week ago Cain conferred with a federal official here while making the rounds of crime syndicate hangouts as a courier for exiled mob boss Sam (Momo) Giancana, it was learned."

The lowdown on Cain, offered "privately" to the million or so readers of one of the largest metropolitan dailies in the country, may have been what intelligence operatives call disinformation. Neither federal authorities nor their aides ordinarily identify informants, even dead ones. It discourages potential informers. And if Cain had indeed conferred with the feds a week before he was killed, why tell the press about it? Blowing Cain's cover renders any information he might have provided useless.

Nor was there anything new about the allegations. Cain was notorious for working both sides of the street. It was public knowledge that he consorted with mobsters while working for the Chicago police and the Cook County sheriff. Columnists in the Chicago papers routinely referred to him as "two-faced" and a "double agent." He didn't shrink from those appellations. On the contrary, he reveled in the notoriety they gave him. But suddenly, after he was assassinated, the double life he had lived for more than 20 years was offered up as the mob's motive for killing him.

More tidbits dropped by unidentified federal sources are scattered throughout the many articles concerning Cain that appeared after his death, among them this one: "Cain left Mexico two months ago, and federal agents who keep watch on the movements of hoodlums believe he was on a mission for Sam Giancana."

No one was arrested for the murder of Cain, and to the extent that anyone remembers it now, it is considered a mob killing. Two years later, Giancana was assassinated on the day Senate Intelligence Committee staffers arrived in Chicago to arrange for testimony he had finally agreed to give. His death prompted open speculation that he had been murdered to preclude that testimony.

The intelligence community wanted both Cain and Giancana either dead or out of subpoena range, especially Cain. It was widely understood that Cain could spill the beans on CIA activities dating back to the 1950s. Giancana stayed put in Mexico until shortly before he was killed, but Cain was forever popping in and out of Chicago, a habit that would have resulted in his death years earlier if the mob truly wanted to kill him. A lone gunman with a Mafia contract (the typical mob MO) would have nailed him the first time he showed his face in a place like Rose's Sandwich Shop, a mob hangout he was known to frequent.

But a hit squad of seven people (two killers, the woman in black, and the four men Cain came to the sandwich shop to meet) couldn't strike that fast. They would need ample lead time, which would require keeping track of Cain's travels and prior knowledge that he was heading for Chicago.

The newspapers speculated that Giancana had fingered him, which made sense. They'd been told "by unidentified federal sources" that Cain had been on a mission for Giancana until shortly before his death, so he would have known Cain's whereabouts and his plans.

* * *

Sometime during their extended stay on the isle of Guadeloupe it must have occurred to the Frenchmen that they had hijacked the wrong boat. An amazing array of U.S. government agencies were trying to find evidence of piracy and murder to use against them. Cables and courier-delivered letters flew back and forth across the Caribbean, many of them by way of the U.S. State Department.

The FBI alone had four offices working on the matter: the foreign liaison unit, a legal attaché based in Caracas, the Miami office, and the Mexico City office. The Canal Zone offices of naval intelligence and the Office of Strategic Information were both assisting the effort. The American embassy in Paris served as a liaison between the Paris police and investigators on Guadeloupe. It was the embassy's efforts that unearthed a warrant for one of the Frenchmen's arrest on a draft evasion charge.

Many of the memos in the file concern searches and inquiries that had "negative results," but anything that might indicate where those searches took place, or what the inquiries concerned (with one exception), is blacked out.

The U.S. attorney in Miami, Laurence Craig, is copied on everything. Several documents refer to Craig's insistence that he cannot prosecute the Frenchmen without more evidence. A January 1975 memo to the FBI director's office states: "Craig has advised that based on the facts known to date there is no evidence of a crime on the high seas. While Seymour and Breckenridge appear to be missing, there is no corpus delicti or other evidence of death."

A related inquiry into the fate of the U.S.-registered yacht Royal Star III and the French yacht St. Georges was opened.

The documents concerning those boats are heavily censored, but apparently they are the other two vessels the Frenchmen hijacked. A March 15, 1974, memo from the FBI's legal attaché in Caracas raises the possibility that Breckenridge was involved in one of those hijackings: "Inquiries are underway to determine if Breckenridge was a crew member aboard the Royal Star III at the time of the crime, or whether he went aboard as caretaker after the yacht was brought from Santa Marta to Cartagena," says the memo.

It all came to nothing though. About a year after the Frenchmen were seized, a cablegram from Paris advised the U.S. attorney in Miami that one of them could be held indefinitely on a draft evasion charge if that was his pleasure. U.S. Attorney Craig didn't acknowledge the suggestion. He merely advised the FBI's legal attaché in Caracas, on May 6, 1975, that he was declining prosecution. He cites the lack of hard evidence, which made it extremely unlikely that either man could be convicted.

There remained only one impediment to the Frenchmen's release. A few days later they appeared in court in Pointe-A-Pitre. The magistrate asked them again, for the record, if they claimed ownership of the Immamou. They answered no, and he told them they were free to go.

* * *

By the time Danny disappeared, rumors about him were nothing new in Minneapolis. Hearsay about his adventures had been filtering back for years—from New York, where he was at the center of a circle of photographers and filmmakers; from Spain, where he was living in a cave and making a film about flamenco music; from London, where he was dating an Australian movie star; from Switzerland, where he and Keith Richards had checked into a clinic to have their blood purified.

Sometimes he would appear in town to offer up some token of his amazing knack. A bunch of Danny's Minneapolis friends were his guests at a backstage party when the Rolling Stones played Met Stadium in 1972. That same summer he showed his film about Lennon and Ono in the backyard of a house on Irving Avenue in Minneapolis. People remembered those occasions when the veracity of gossip about him seemed questionable. Anything can happen when it comes to Danny, was their attitude.

Rumors flew even thicker after he disappeared, each one more melodramatic and unlikely than the last, but in broad outline they proved to be pretty accurate. Somehow a few snippets of fact had made it through the barrier that George Gardner erected, and friends who had been hearing about Danny's escapades for years used them to intuit the rest. It couldn't have been a simple misadventure, or even a bloody example of modern piracy. It had to be connected to some of the central dramas of the times: cold war politics, the CIA/Mafia axis, the assassination of John F. Kennedy.

Eventually, wishful thinking superseded intuition, and Danny was resurrected. He'd been seen walking the beach in San Blas. Somebody spotted him splashing around in a lagoon in the Dutch Antilles. He had kicked heroin, chucked his inheritance, and grown a beard. He was making a new life for himself in the islands.

Only one rumor met the barest standards of plausibility. It had a few brush strokes of detail that rang true, and a second-hand source, a Minneapolitan named Chris Hamley, who had done a stretch in a Mexican prison in the late 1970s. Hamley's cell mate was another gringo, and the two of them passed time swapping stories. Hamley told about Danny's disappearance.

His cell mate knew of the case. He had spent some time on Guadeloupe during the Frenchmen's stay there.

According to him, the Frenchmen reasoned that their fate depended on how well they could pass as innocent sailors, so instead of hiring a competent attorney, they told the magistrate that they were broke, and settled for the colonial equivalent of a public defender, a law clerk who made a month-long project out of getting them released from the island's dungeon-like jail.

According to Hamley's cell mate, it took nerve and re-solve to go through with that plan. A good solicitor could have sprung them with a few phone calls, and they could have hired one. It was common knowledge in some circles that they had plenty of money stashed in Martinique.

Once they got out of jail, they had to watch themselves carefully. They were in the public eye. The story they told of the legal nightmare that befell them when they tried to help two strung out Americans, plus the aura of danger that hung about them, combined to make them celebrities. Especially the Corsican-looking one. He cut a wide swath through the ladies of Pointe-A-Pitre's yachting set during his months of confinement to the island. Nothing could help his pug-nosed pal in that department though, so both of them lived off the Corsican's conquests while they feigned poverty.

By early 1975, it was apparent that they would soon be released, but they had to play their parts out to the end. That meant they would need to hitchhike a boat ride to Martinique when the court freed them. According to Hamley's cell mate, many a wry joke was made about the brave soul who would dare take them aboard. In the end it was a woman. She and the Corsican had gotten cozy as their departure from Guadeloupe grew imminent.

She was dark-haired and sexy, according to Hamley's cell mate, about thirty-five, olive-skinned, living on a yacht with two men he took to be gay because of their disinterest in the affair she was having. One of them rarely showed his face on shore. The other was more outgoing, a drinker, one of those strange people who have given themselves to the sun. He was middle-aged, but his face looked like a road map etched in rawhide.

The day of the Frenchmen's departure finally came, after an evening of drinks in a tavern and fond farewells all around. Hamley's cell mate was on the dock with the others. They watched the boat glide slowly out of port, the Corsican on deck with an arm around his new lover, his putty-nosed partner standing nearby, smiling a pinched little smile, and the leather man at the helm.

A few months later Hamley's cell mate saw the sun worshiper again, in a bar in Trinidad. Being a little drunk and feeling garrulous, he greeted him thusly: "Well, I see you survived your cruise with the pirates."

The man cocked his head, quizzically. "What do you mean?" he said.

"You know, the Frenchmen. The ones who sailed with you, from Pointe-a-Pitre."

"I have no idea what you're talking about," he replied. "You have me confused with someone else."

His tone was polite enough, but something in his stare made Hamley's cell mate agree that he was indeed confused, even though he knew he wasn't. The man locked eyes with him for a few more moments. Then he picked up his drink and walked to the other end of the bar.

Not long before Danny was reported missing, his half-sister, Rosa Van Kirk, was beaten almost to death in New York. She suffered brain damage and spent the rest of her life in an institution.

Isabella Gardner's health declined rapidly after her children's misfortunes, but she continued to write. In 1979, she published a collection of new and selected poems titled *That Was Then*, which was nominated for the National Book Award. The new work in the book concerns people she had loved, or who had been important in her life. One is dedicated to George Gardner, the brother with whom she had always felt a special bond.

These lines are from the title poem, in which she reminisces about summer days on the beach with her children:

My daughter then five, now in
Bedlam, chased butterflies and thirty years ago my infant son,
now for some years lost, was happy too. I washed his diapers

George Gardner was loathe to have his nephew declared officially dead while his sister was alive, but soon after her death in 1981 he did so, and Danny's estate was divided. It consisted of films, photographs, and possessions, but very little cash. Gardner hired a crew to bring Danny's boat to Boston, where it was sold.

When George Gardner was queried about his relationship with Richard Cain for this story, he replied, "I have nothing to tell you about that."

Welcome to Pine County

Welcome to Pine County

Welcome to Pine County

This is an amalgam of a couple of stories about a situation that developed in a rural area north of the Twin Cities in the mid-1990s. Sketchy characters from urban centers were showing up there because it seemed so remote and inaccessible. It made for some strange encounters between them, local residents and law enforcement.

On February 20, 1996, the Pine County sheriff's office received a call from a man who identified himself as Chuck Strobel. He said there were intruders on his property. "Hurry," he implored the desk officer. "They're in the house right now!"

His plea stirred no sense of urgency at the sheriff's office. Strobel had reported burglaries in progress on many other occasions, and they'd all turned out to be false alarms. Deputies had once responded to a claim that Martians had landed in Strobel's yard and were peeking in the window. The only call from his residence that turned out to have a factual basis came earlier that year, when Strobel was arrested for assault on a complaint by his girlfriend.

A former Minneapolis resident, Strobel had been living in an old house on 20 acres in a remote area south of Hinckley, Minnesota, about 80 miles north of the Twin Cities, for four years. He was an antique dealer who specialized in restoring furniture.

Although he'd taken great pains to isolate himself, he seemed to be spooked by being alone. He informed the officers who responded to one of his early calls that he'd set "man-traps" consisting of spring-loaded shotguns around his property, and that he was prepared to shoot anyone who tried to enter his house forcibly. Nevertheless, deputies Jared Rosati and Steven Ovick were dispatched to check out the latest invasion of Strobel's privacy.

Strobel, agitated and babbling, met them in the yard. He said that four Hell's Angels had broken into his house. Since he'd earlier claimed that these same bikers had obtained copies of his keys and were making themselves at home in his absence, the deputies were skeptical. They asked why the intruders hadn't just opened the door and walked in. Strobel didn't know why, but he was sure they were robbing him blind at that very moment. He explained that they'd tunneled into the basement, then had managed to sneak up to the second floor past him and his dog before he heard them stomping around up there.

Deputy Rosati noticed a handgun tucked into Strobel's belt. "We'll go in and check it out," he said, "but give me that pistol first." Strobel handed over the weapon, then led the officers on a tour of the premises. There was nobody inside, nor was there any sign of forced entry. The last room they approached was Strobel's bedroom.

"He told our officers to stay the hell out of there," says Lt. Robert Johnson, an investigator with the Pine County Sheriff's Department until his recent retirement. "That kind of piqued their interest, but they really had no right to go in if he didn't want them to."

The officers terminated what was obviously a fruitless search for intruders. "The next time you call us, don't be carrying any weapons when we arrive," said Rosati. "Understand?"

* * *

Murder in Minneapolis made the front page of the New York Times in the mid-1990s because gang wars over drug turf resulted in a rash of killings, but rural Minnesota is where the crime rate really climbed in those years. Between 1990 and 1995 total violent crimes reported by rural sheriff's departments increased 12 percent, while Minneapolis actually recorded a tiny decrease. Pine County has seen more than its share of criminal activity. Too far away to function as a bedroom community and too desolate for tourism, it seems to strike some metro thugs as the ideal location to avoid scrutiny. "We're getting a different type up here now," says Johnson.

They are city-bred criminals, who often combine a high level of sophistication about their line of work with some naive expectations concerning rural Minnesota. Maybe it's the "portal zones" that fool them. Dense forest borders the gravel roads of Pine County, but it's only the quarter mile of illusion the loggers leave after they haul the woods away to make paper. Nevertheless, driving through a gauntlet of trees miles from the nearest town seems to foster fantasies of isolation among criminally inclined ex-urbanites.

Some adopt a reclusive lifestyle that has its own way of drawing the neighbors' attention. Others act as if nothing they do matters because they are so far from anywhere. In reality, their lifestyle makes them more visible than they would ever be in a city. Either way, they are armed and dangerous.

In mid-October, an outdoor marijuana-growing operation was discovered in rural Pine County. "I can't give you the suspect's name because we haven't picked him up yet," says Deputy Thomas Pitzen. "I can tell you he's a biker-gang member, and a white supremacist. He didn't have any of the kind of monitoring equipment we often run into up here, but he was certainly well armed. We discovered a shooting range and lots of expended shells on the property."

Pitzen was part of an eight-man SWAT team that responded to a report of a disturbance in Sturgeon Lake. A woman named Marlys Koza had called the sheriff to say that her boyfriend, Greg Padden, was fighting with a man named Randy Fett. Moments later a second call came, this one from Fett's son, who said his father had been shot.

The SWAT team found Fett, 38, dead in the road. He'd been shot in the shoulder and the head. Koza and other witnesses said an argument had broken out while Fett was discussing the purchase of a trailer from Padden.

"It was a beef between a couple drunks, metro-area transplants," says Pitzen. "We arrested Padden in the woods about a mile away. I'd like to say that kind of thing is unheard of up here, but unfortunately it isn't. That's why we've put together the SWAT team." Padden has been charged with second-degree murder.

According to Johnson, city criminals most often use rural areas like Pine County to establish safe houses where they hide out and store drugs for major transactions. "Sometimes they conduct their business up here, but more often their activities are in the city and this is a retreat. Are they successful? Well, let's put it this way. I only hear about the unsuccessful ones."

The most flamboyantly unsuccessful operation in Pine County history was a joint venture between a Chicago branch of the Latin Kings, and members of the Pluff clan of St. Paul's East Side. Their alliance was forged in 1988, when Cindy Pluff, who'd run away from home at 16 to become a prostitute, met a Colombian cocaine dealer in Las Vegas. He introduced her to his Chicago distributor, Jose Rodriguez, a.k.a. "Cabeza," a reference to the brainy way he organized the cocaine trade on that city's North Side.

Rodriguez lost his cabeza over Cindy Pluff. They moved in together, and his monthly trade with the Colombians increased substantially. By 1989, Cindy had become the major cocaine distributor in the Twin Cities, with headquarters at the Pluff family home on East Magnolia Street in St. Paul. Cindy lived in Chicago with Cabeza, but the stress and strain of the cocaine trade made them yearn for some place remote to chill out. With that in mind, she and Rodriguez purchased an old farmhouse on 55 wooded acres, on Pine County Road 32. Cindy's father, Kenneth Pluff Sr., became the caretaker.

Cindy, Cabeza, some other Latin Kings, plus the Pluff gang and their chief clients began spending long weekends there in the summer of 1988. By then Rodriguez had become too fond of his product, the kiss of death in the cocaine racket and particularly hazardous in his organization because he kept the books in his fabled cabeza.

In July 1988, Rodriguez traveled to the farm with two nephews and a friend from Miami, Orlando Guirola, whose usual chore was preparing cocaine for Rodriguez to free-base. Late on the day they arrived, Rodriguez smoked a pipe Guirola gave him and had a seizure. He was brought unconscious to the Sandstone hospital emergency room and died a few hours later. Management of his organization defaulted to Rudy Martinez, a colleague of Cabeza's whose responsibilities had previously consisted of collecting overdue bills from street dealers.

Martinez was barely 22 when Rodriguez's scrambled affairs landed in his lap. His relationship with Pluff mimicked Rodriguez's: mostly business, plus some casual sex. Over the next 18 months, the situation in Pine County became more and more frenzied. A virtual Who's Who of cocaine distribution in the Twin Cities came to and from the farm, all of them apparently oblivious to the fact that they were under intense scrutiny by their neighbors and local law enforcement.

"We didn't know what was going on when they first started coming here," says former Sheriff Don Faulkner, "but they did get our attention. The death of Mr. Rodriguez was the first major incident, but there were many others."

Opinions vary on when local residents realized they had something extraordinary in their midst. It might have been Thanksgiving Day, 1989, when the neighbors down the road, Elmer and Shirley Ellgren, heard a terrible ruckus at the Pluff farm. "It sounded like an invasion or something," says Shirley Ellgren.

Actually, it was the ritual slaughter of the Thanksgiving bird, Latin Kings style, an event memorialized on videotape that would later be scrutinized by the police. Rudy Martinez dispatched the turkey, a huge tom, with a quick burst from an AK-47 assault rifle, then celebrated the kill by firing a few hundred rounds into the air.

"I guess I can see why the Elmers, or whatever their names are, might have been upset," Martinez later acknowledged. "We could've been a lot cooler, but we didn't think people would take notice. It seemed like we were all alone up there."

Martinez also confesses to being chagrined about another incident. It was deer-hunting season, and one sunny afternoon Elmer Ellgren headed for the blind he'd built in a tree on his property, his old lever-action 30-30 over his shoulder. But when he arrived, the blind was occupied. Up in Ellgren's tree was a young man with a Zapata mustache, and an AK-47. Outgunned but undaunted, Ellgren demanded to know what was going on.

Angry words were exchanged, but not fully understood, because Ellgren spoke the rural Minnesota vernacular while the erstwhile hunter expressed himself mostly in Spanglish. Eventually the point was made, and the intruder trudged off toward the adjoining Pluff acreage, exactly where Ellgren thought he'd come from.

By late 1990, hundreds of complaints about the goings-on at the Pluff farm had been logged at the Pine County sheriff's office. The main sources of annoyance were noise, gunfire, and a pack of marauding dogs living on the property. But neighbors had also become suspicious of Ken Pluff's ostentatious displays of wealth. He routinely dropped hundreds of dollars on pull tabs at a bar in Duxbury, a few miles from the farm. His visitors from Chicago also patronized area bars, where they kept mostly to themselves but attracted plenty of attention anyway.

"If I was a drug dealer I'd keep a low profile," says Shirley Ellgren, a feisty lady in her 70s, "but they were just obnoxious. You wouldn't believe the loud music, the gunfire, cars coming and going. And boy did they party—nonstop."

Residents wondered why they had to put with it. They didn't know that the Pine County sheriff's office had become part of a multi-agency task force that was planning a major bust at the Pluff farm and elsewhere. On January 19, 1991, simultaneous raids were carried out at the Pluff home in St. Paul, a stash house on Chicago's North Side, and the farm. Officers from the state Bureau of Criminal Apprehension, the federal Drug Enforcement Administration, the Treasury Department, the state Highway Patrol, and the Pine County sheriff's office—25 law-enforcement officers in all—descended on the Pluff farm.

"Oh, you should have seen it," says Mrs. Ellgren. "They came with helicopters, cars with their lights flashing, men with flak jackets and big guns. It was wonderful. It was just like Miami Vice!"

More than 30 people were arrested in the three raids. The Pluff family and a few of their Twin Cities colleagues were indicted in St. Paul. The others faced trial in Chicago. A possible 20 years in prison loomed for many defendants, including Rudy Martinez and Cindy Pluff. An open question was whether Pluff would be charged under the Chicago or St. Paul indictment. Both were for conspiracy to distribute, but the St. Paul indictment alleged a much smaller quantity and the potential sentences were commensurately shorter.

Prosecutors immediately began offering deals, but it took a while to make them. The trials did not begin for almost two years. The number who were willing to testify in return for plea bargains astounded DEA agents.

"That family in Minnesota kind of hung together and said to hell with everybody else," an investigator in Chicago says. According to Martinez's attorney, Richard Kling, there was no shortage of snitches, but there were only two who could provide the comprehensive testimony the prosecution wanted: Rudy Martinez and Cindy Pluff.

Martinez was the real prize, but he couldn't be turned. He and Pluff were locked up at the Metropolitan Correctional Center (MCC), a federal holding facility in Chicago, while they awaited trial. The MCC has separate wings for men and women, but Pluff and Martinez still managed to communicate.

"She would send me messages that she would never co-operate with the government," Martinez says. "Actually, she'd already begun cooperating, with the Bureau of Criminal Apprehension (BCA) in Minnesota and the Drug Enforcement Agency (DEA) in Chicago."

In April 1991, Cindy sat down with DEA agents and gave up the names of 39 suppliers and customers. In return, she was added to the St. Paul indictment. A little less than a year later, after she'd testified against Martinez and several other defendants, she was sentenced to seven-and-a-half years and sent to a women's prison in California to serve her time. Her father, mother, brothers and sisters received what amounted to slaps on the wrist.

The bargain she made required her to lie about her dealings with Martinez. The U.S. Attorney had offered Martinez a "blind plea": no cooperation required, accept full responsibility for the 20 kilos, and receive a sentence of 15 to 20 years, possibly mitigated by the fact that it would be his first conviction.

"I told my attorney that I would take that deal," says Martinez. "But when we went to see the prosecutor, he offered me a different deal, eight years, if I cooperated. I refused."

Three days later, a superseding indictment was handed down. Martinez was accused of participating in a "Continuing Criminal Enterprise," a broad statute under which felonies in a variety of areas—financial fraud, racketeering, drug offenses, etc.—can be charged. The sentencing protocol for this statute allows for aggravating factors that can lead to stiffer penalties. The section pertaining to drugs mandates a life sentence for anyone found guilty of distributing "at least 300 times the quantity of a substance described in subsection 401(b)." For cocaine, the base amount under this statute is 500 grams. Multiplied by 300, that equals 150 kilos. The government accused Martinez of distributing at least that amount, and with Cindy Pluff's help, convinced a jury that he'd done so.

Two falsehoods formed the basis for his conviction: Pluff's courtroom admission that her family sold in excess of 150 kilos of cocaine during the period of the conspiracy, which was a wild exaggeration; and her testimony that Martinez was her sole supplier, which was an outright lie. Pluff has since admitted that in both instances she lied under oath. At the time, however, those perjuries taken together required the judge to sentence Martinez to mandatory life under federal sentencing guidelines.

Soon after Cindy Pluff began serving her 7 ½-year sentence she was sent to Chicago to testify against another defendant who was on trial for a different cocaine conspiracy. She was being housed at the Chicago MCC, waiting to go to court, when she became involved in a sting operation targeting guards who were having sex with female inmates. Her efforts in that matter earned her a further reduction, and she was released, having served less than two years of her original sentence.

* * *

The Pluff family saga built to a crescendo about the time Minneapolis residents Charles Strobel and his girlfriend Diane Roy began yearning for some rural solitude.

According to his fellow antique dealers, Strobel was a shy, gentle person, and a meticulous craftsman. He smoked marijuana constantly, but Roy claims he never used crack or other drugs when they lived in Minneapolis.

The couple bought and sold large furniture. Strobel restored many of the pieces himself. "He was an artist," says a manager at the Cobblestone Antique co-op in Minneapolis, where Strobel and Roy had a booth. "It takes talent to restore furniture."

It also takes methylene chloride, the key ingredient in furniture stripper. Thus, in addition to smoking copious amounts of marijuana, and breathing the usual urban cocktail of carbon monoxide, benzene fugitives, secondary formaldehyde, arsenic, chloroform, and on down the list of ubiquitous air pollutants, Strobel was inhaling one of the most lethal of all industrial chemicals.

An eight-hour average of 100 parts per million of methylene chloride is the maximum exposure a human being can tolerate without sustaining severe harm. Since its odor threshold is 300 parts per million, if you smell it, it's too late. According to the federal Centers for Disease Control, the only ways to provide protection from the chemical are very well-ventilated workspaces or full-face breathing masks with their own air supply. The lungs, liver, kidney, and brain are the primary target organs of volatilized methylene chloride. Symptoms of acute exposure include giddiness, confusion, and delirium. Symptoms of chronic exposure are imperfectly understood, but grave.

In 1992, Diane Roy purchased an old house on 20 acres in Pine County. At first she and Strobel stayed there together, but by 1994 Strobel was a permanent resident and Roy had become an infrequent visitor.

"I stopped going up there because he went nuts," she would later tell investigators. "He'd started hitting me and abusing me. He'd never done that before. He was a good man. But he was drinking a lot, and doing drugs."

During a visit she made in the autumn of 1995, Roy noticed that Strobel had installed heavy duty doors with steel frames. The windows, including those in his workroom, were nailed shut.

Valuable items Roy was storing in the house gradually disappeared. Strobel said they'd been stolen. "He was always talking about thieves," Roy explained. "He said people were coming around to rob him. Then he started accusing me of robbing him, and I hadn't even been up there."

Strobel placed video cameras in several rooms, and in a pole barn he'd erected. When Roy inquired about two large holes in an interior wall, apparently made by shotgun blasts, he made another vague reference to thieves.

In January 1996, Strobel accused Roy of helping the Hell's Angels rob him. "He said I was the one who gave them the keys to the place," she told investigators. "I think he's gone, you know, paranoid."

Early in the morning of February 23, three days after begging deputies to rid his house of imaginary robbers, Chuck Strobel called the Pine County sheriff again. He'd spotted several bikers prowling around his yard. They'd driven up in a large, four-door vehicle.

"Keep him on the line, and tell him not to have any weapons when we get there," Deputy Pitzen instructed the dispatcher. "Tell him everything is cool. Just wait for us, then come out in the yard unarmed."

A state Highway Patrol sergeant named Thomas Ceiluch offered to join Pitzen and Deputy Jared Rosati for backup. The moment the officers arrived it was clear that no one had preceded them to the property. Fresh snow had fallen, and there were no tire tracks or footprints.

"Chuck came running out toward us," says Pitzen. "He was pointing at Tom Ceiluch, and yelling, 'Good, you finally got him! Let me see who he is!' As near as I could tell he thought that Tom was one of the Hell's Angels who were tunneling into his house, and we'd arrested him."

Rosati ordered Strobel to halt. In the dim dawn light the officers could see that Strobel had an electric cord with multiple plugs and a surge protector tied around his waist. He had a file in one hand and a knife in the other. When Pitzen told him to raise his hands, Rosati spotted a pistol tucked under the cord.

"We told you not to have any weapons," said Pitzen. "I'm going to pat you down now to make sure you don't have anything else." He found four shotgun shells and a bag of what looked like crack cocaine in Strobel's shirt pocket. "That's when we arrested him," he says. "We asked if the cocaine was his, and he just said, 'Yeah, it's mine.'"

The officers handcuffed Strobel and were about to drive off to Pine City with him when he asked if they would please put his dog in the house.

"In other words," says Pitzen, "he invited us in." Barely inside, the officers spotted a bag of marijuana, a cooking spoon, and a homemade crack pipe. They secured the dog and headed for Pine City to process Strobel and get a search warrant.

Strobel seemed calm on the way. He volunteered that he'd had a bunch of buddies over the previous night to test his cocaine. It was a damning admission if true, but the deputies had their doubts due to the lack of tracks or footprints. When Diane Roy was questioned, she was asked whether Strobel might have had friends in to snort cocaine. "What friends?" she replied. "He doesn't have any friends."

When the officers returned to the house with a search warrant, they discovered what Strobel had been telling them about in his own strange way for two years. His place was a veritable treasure trove of familiar controlled substances, scattered amid the less familiar paraphernalia of chemically induced paranoia. The search proceeded cautiously. "We were worried about all those spring guns and booby traps he'd been telling us about," says Pitzen.

The smell of weed permeated the house so thoroughly that a drug-sniffing dog had to be pulled away from the heat ducts and guided into more promising venues.

There were two locked safes. One contained a small bag of powder cocaine and reams of video-surveillance tape. The other held $4,200 in cash and 80 pounds of marijuana. Between that and a stash in the bedroom a total of 218 pounds of pot was discovered. Shotgun holes were blasted through the walls and the door of a closet. The officers seized more than 20 guns, ranging in size from a .22-caliber two-shot derringer to a .375-caliber Magnum rifle suitable for hunting elephants. They also found a Safe House Wireless Security Scanner, three surveillance cameras and various viewing devices.

Investigators were later able to determine that Strobel hadn't slept for more than 72 hours when he was arrested. Dozens of pills including codeine and various uppers were seized during the search. So were the untagged pelts of several animals. Keys, door locks, and tumblers were piled on a table, and there were signs that the locks had been changed many times.

"Maybe he wanted to get caught," Pitzen says. "Either that or he just lost track of who he was talking to."

Strobel was charged with nine counts of controlled-substance violations and four counts based on his possession of wild-animal pelts. In return for his plea of guilty to one count of possession of marijuana with intent to sell, all the other charges were dropped. On October 31, 1996, he received a 38-month sentence with a recommendation that he be considered for a program that would put him on the street in less than two years. The prosecutor chose to ignore the guns in Strobel's possession.

One theory that was kicked around the squad room for a while concerned the possibility that Strobel was indeed connected to the Hell's Angels, and was holding up the orderly flow of marijuana from Point A to Point B in that organization's distribution chain. Thus, it was theorized, he had come to think of prison as his best option, a kind of safe house away from the safe house.

"I don't think he was connected to anybody," says Johnson. "The Pluffs were different. They were part of a large organization. Strobel was more representative. He was a loner. That's the type we often see up here.

"Was he dangerous? Well, better than half the weapons he had were loaded, and there was some pretty high-test weaponry there. There was a high-quality night scope mounted on a 44 Desert Eagle, for example, and a pistol with a scope on it. That thing was so big and heavy I don't see how a person could aim it unless you set it on something. He could have definitely shot through our vests."

Apparently it was sheer chance that he didn't. "When we first locked him up, he told the jailer that he'd had our officers in his sights as they drove up his driveway," says Johnson. "He just decided not to shoot for whatever reason. I guess he just drifted off into some other hallucination."

Star Stalker

Star Stalker

This story was published in *Chicago Magazine* in 1992. The possibility that Ralph Nau might be released from custody was real, and Hollywood security agent Gavin de Becker, normally a hard man for journalists to talk to, was very cooperative. Several of his clients wanted to make sure Nau remained behind bars. The term "Stalker" was just entering the language at that time.

The letters started coming to singer/actress Olivia Newton-John in 1982—bizarre, rambling screeds, alternately pathetic and frightening, sexually explicit, written by someone who signed different names. Newton-John hired a Hollywood security firm, which eventually traced the letters to a young Midwesterner named Ralph Nau. The firm started monitoring

Nau's whereabouts, and urged his family to get him psychiatric help. But otherwise it could do nothing. Nau's letters talked of death and killings, and they were intimate and intimidating, but he hadn't broken any laws.

Then, in 1984, while Nau was living with his mother and stepfather on a farm near Antioch, Illinois, his autistic eight-year-old stepbrother was murdered with an ax. Though the evidence strongly suggested that Nau, in the grip of a severe delusion, had killed the boy, and though he made what seemed to be a confession, he was found mentally unfit for trial. At a later hearing a judge decided there was insufficient evidence to continue holding him as a murder suspect. At that point, for all intents and purposes, he was a free man. Only demands by outraged prosecutors to put him in a state hospital kept him off the streets.

Today, Ralph Nau, 48, is still in a state hospital. He spends most of his time watching television and sending letters to movie and television stars. Over the years these have included Newton-John, Cher, Sheena Easton, and several Chicago newscasters who he's convinced send him "love vibes" through the TV screen. He's sure they are all in love with him, and were they not prevented by supernatural forces, would rush to his side. Before he was committed, he traveled to Hollywood and to Newton-John's native Australia, seeking to be closer to the objects of his obsessions. There's no reason to assume that he wouldn't go to Hollywood, Australia or Chicago to search them out again if he had the chance.

He may get it. Nau keeps petitioning for release, and he may eventually win. His story raises difficult questions about what should qualify as a crime, and of how to deal with someone who is profoundly troubled. When he was free there was no law in Illinois against obsessive attention toward someone, against "stalking" them. The phenomenon, especially directed at celebrities, was so strange the legal system hadn't learned to deal with it. His case raised fundamental questions. How do you distinguish between a fan's ardor and a schizophrenic's delusions? What marks the boundary between the attention that celebrities invite, even crave, and a dangerous obsession?

"Erotomania is hardly a new affliction," says Park Dietz, a forensic psychiatrist in Newport Beach, California, who has done extensive research on erotomania and celebrities. "There were case studies of it written a century ago. But conditions in today's culture certainly have led to a greater instance of it. Loneliness, alienation, an inability to connect to others all contribute to the creation of erotomanic delusions. Of course, most cases don't involve celebrities. They involve the girl next door or in the next office."

Nor do they necessarily involve stalking. True erotomaniacs are convinced that the person they have fixated upon loves them in return. But not all of them require proof of that. For some, it's enough to simply stare at the person they love or write letters. The problems come in those cases where the erotomaniac decides to make himself known to the woman he loves and get evidence of her love in return. The net result is sometimes violent. Dietz cites the cases of John Hinckley, Jr., who shot President Reagan in a deluded effort to impress actress Jodie Foster, and Arthur Jackson, who tried to kill actress Teresa Saldana.

Ralph Nau has never been accused of hurting any of the women he's stalked. In fact, most people who have known Nau have thought him relatively normal. He graduated from high school. He's held responsible jobs. He's always refused any offers of counseling or help.

To be released, he needs to show convincingly that he is improving, that he's no longer a clear danger to himself or others. "I'm afraid he'll be out someday," says Randall Stewart, who unsuccessfully prosecuted Nau for murder in 1984.

Other people are afraid as well. At one point, Newton-John, Cher, and Sheena Easton issued a joint public statement: "Ralph Nau has dangerous delusions about us. He has acted on those delusions by traveling great distances to pursue us, so we are understandably concerned about the safety of our families and our own safety. We see a greater need for concern, however, in the community where he has killed before, and where he has a continuing relationship to potential victims. This is where the decisions are made that will affect the peace of mind and safety of possible future victims, and this is where public concern can make a difference."

The Lesson

Ralph Nau was born July 1, 1955, to a farm family in rural Wisconsin. While he was growing up, his father, Delmar Nau, belonged to a "Swing Club" with some of his rural Wisconsin neighbors. "My parents had a very active sex life," Ralph Nau recently wrote in a letter to this author. "Often they went to bed with other couples. A few times they had sex parties. Sometimes I got a glimpse of it going on."

It was more than a glimpse, according to the recollections of other family members. Ralph, his older sister, Lorrie, and his younger brother, Kerry, slept on the second floor of the Nau house, an area heated through a vent that allowed a clear view of the room below. Ralph sometimes watched while his parents and the other swingers swung on the first floor.

Ralph's sister-in-law, Cissie, who's married to Kerry, knows the family's history well. "Delmar was the instigator of everything that went on. Shirley (his wife) just went along," she says.

Delmar also had a large collection of pornography magazines, which were readily available to his children. "At a very early age," Ralph wrote in another letter for this article, "me and my brother were looking at sex pitchurs, which led to a few silly moments in bed."

This behavior seems to have worried Ralph's father. "Delmar apparently thought Ralph should learn about sex by doing instead of telling," Cissie says. Delmar arranged a "lesson" for his son, which consisted of Ralph having sexual intercourse with his mother. It was a lesson Ralph, who was 16 at the time, remembered well: "I said to myself I'll never do it again with a woman," he wrote, "unless I love her."

Shortly after the lesson, Ralph started writing letters. They began with what his sister Lorrie calls "a crush" on Cher, which prompted an outpouring of fan letters addressed to her. These were ardent but ordinary missives, but there were other hints in Nau's behavior: An excellent hunter and a crack shot, he allegedly began killing small animals during this time, mutilating them, and burying them around the farm. Still, to most people he appeared to be a normal, unexceptional young man. "He was never a troublemaker," says Jerome Binsfeld, Nau's counselor at Central High School in Paddock Lake, Wisconsin. He earned average grades and graduated in 1974.

A year later, he came across an ad in a pornography magazine that invited readers to join a club. Members were allowed to correspond with their pick from a photo gallery of sexy women. He signed up, and suddenly Cher took a back seat to his new interest, pen-name Candy. He would spend his days working on the farm, and his evenings composing long, passionate letters to Candy, often enclosing small sums of money. He also corresponded occasionally with a woman at the club named Maria.

"Maria" seems to have been a device to chasten correspondents whose letters were too obscene, thus jeopardizing the club's legal standing. One of the threats Maria used was to cut off correspondence privileges. She assumed a position of power in Nau's mind.

In 1980, at the age of 25, Nau decided he wanted to meet Candy in person. He borrowed $1,300 from his father and headed for Peoria, where Candy's post-office box was located. There he was told that all correspondence was forwarded to an address in Phoenix.

Nau immediately left for Arizona. His search for Candy was futile, but he later told psychiatrists (according to a source familiar with his psychiatric records) that during his wanderings in Arizona a mysterious being called Maria revealed herself to him. She told him that he and Cher, and he and Olivia Newton-John, were soul mates, and she instructed him to go to Los Angeles to pursue his relationships with both women.

Not long after his arrival in Los Angeles, Maria apparently showed Nau how capricious she could be. She turned on him, he told psychiatrists later, bewitching Newton-John and Cher, and preventing them from responding to his advances. Nau began having visions in which both women turned into vicious animals and attacked him. Gradually his interest began to focus on Newton-John almost exclusively, and the tempo of his letter writing increased. When it reached the level of three to five letters a day, Maria took the extreme step of removing

Newton-John from the planet, and replacing her with a dou-ble. This impostor, Nau believed, was as evil as the authentic Newton-John was sweet.

"I am at war with Maria," he wrote to Newton-John in 1981. "You don't know how I want her out of my life. I wish a few people was out of your life also."

Nau found a job as a kennel man at a Los Angeles veterinary clinic called The Cat and Dog Hospital. He was paid $125 a week, plus room and board on the premises. There, among the sick animals and the veterinary paraphernalia, he sank deeper into delusion. He decorated his room with posters, turning it into a shrine to Olivia Newton-John. For companionship he adopted a mutt and named it Sam, after a Newton-John song.

Weird as he was, he carried out his chores conscientious-ly. His employer, Ralph Goodman, remembered him as an excellent worker who took good care of his only friend, his pet dog. He seemed rational and reliable, Goodman recalls. His only quirk was that he talked about Newton-John incessantly, al-ternately referring to her as his wife and his sister. "I tried to get him counseling," says Goodman. "He wouldn't hear of it."

Away from his employer, Nau's behavior became increas-ingly bizarre and, finally, dangerous. He told psychiatrists that he once forced sleeping pills down a sick puppy's throat to kill it, then put it in a freezer with other dead patients. The puppy, he believed, was a bewitched creature sent by Maria to keep him away from Newton-John. "Whoever is in charge of all this shit," he wrote to the singer in 1981, "they're going real low when they start in on a defenseless little puppy. They should all be six feet under." One letter he sent her contained a dog's teeth.

By early 1982, he'd become as obsessed with sing-er Sheena Easton as he was with Newton-John. At one of

Easton's concerts, he was halted by security agents when he tried to reach the stage. Later he wrote a letter to Newton-John describing the experience and blaming it on Maria. "I truly wish I were dead and it would be so easy for me to kill myself if someone didn't do it for me, and I really don't care if they did," he wrote. "I know the name to this game. It's either we go or Maria. Either we die or she and a whole lot more do." He went on to discuss the significance of the numbers 8 and 15, his seat and row numbers at the Easton concert.

"Finding personal significance in coincidental phenomena is called 'referential delusion'," says Dr. Dietz, who's familiar with the Nau case. "That's to distinguish it from delusion that could in fact be true. If someone is convinced his wife is being unfaithful despite evidence to the contrary, that is a delusion. If he sees a blue car followed by a red car, and perceives that as a message that his wife is being unfaithful, that is a referential delusion." If a pattern of referential delusion develops, Dietz says, it can be indicative of profound illness.

By the time Hollywood security agent Gavin de Becker laid eyes on Ralph Nau, he had read hundreds of pages of his writings. They came in the form of letters to de Becker's clients, and they were terrifying, which is why they wound up with de Becker in the first place.

De Becker is a consultant to public figures on safety and privacy matters. Although he refuses to divulge the names of his clients, the reported list of celebrities who pay him more than $200,000 per year is long: Robert Redford, Madonna, Dolly Parton, Tina Turner, and many others. He has a large staff, including experienced investigators. He has scanned 150,000 letters, ranging from the harmless prattle of star-struck fans to the ravings of schizophrenics. His organization has assessed 9,000 cases, more than 1,000 of which he considers dangerous enough to have the individuals monitored.

Nau would have joined this list as early as 1980, when de Becker first read one of his letters—except the letter, to Cher, came with the return address "Xanadu" (the title of one of Newton-John's movies), and was signed "Shawn Newson-John." There were no clues to the writer's real name. De Becker was baffled as the letters kept coming, dozens of them, month after month. De Becker might never have discovered who was sending them if he hadn't added one more client to his list. When Olivia Newton-John signed on with his firm in 1981, she brought along a thick packet of letters from Nau. Many were signed with his real name.

Recognizing that these must be from the same man who'd been writing to Cher, de Becker set about tracking the writer down. By late 1981, he was monitoring the Nau case, and for the next three years, until Nau was arrested for murder in Illinois, de Becker's agents kept track of him. They sat next to him in fast food restaurants, and at Newton-John and Sheena Easton concerts. They struck up conversations with him at work, and on the street. They took pictures of him, questioned people who knew him, and stayed close enough to seize him should he come near any of their clients.

The frightening letters continued to be sent. In a February 1983 letter to Easton, Nau wrote: "They found themselves an impostor for you too, Sheena. If that's true then she better crawl back in her hole with that other one and stay there, to put it mildly." In a letter to Newton-John three months later he wrote: "So it looks like you got me. But it looks like I got you also because if I don't find Olivia I'm as good as dead, and if I die I would hate to see what happens to you."

But de Becker and his agents could not initiate legal action. "Nau was a reliable employee who went to work every day and harmed nobody," says de Becker. "We would have been laughed out of court."

The Cursed Teeth

The Cat and Dog hospital was sold in 1983. The new owners gave Nau a week to find different lodgings. He had saved his money carefully and decided it was time to go to Australia, where he expected Newton-John to be waiting for him at the airport. She wasn't, so he rented a car and drove aimlessly around the countryside looking for her. Days later, dejected at his inability to make contact with Newton-John, he flew back. He returned to his family's farm in Wisconsin in May 1984.

Preparations were under way for the marriage of his younger brother, Kerry, whose wife-to-be, Cissie, came to the farm to discuss wedding plans with her new in-laws the day after Nau arrived. She was told that Ralph was on the second floor, so she went upstairs to meet him. He was unresponsive, until she hit on a topic that animated him.

"My father is a dentist," she explains, "and as soon as I mentioned that, he showed me his teeth, which were badly stained. He wanted to know if my dad could clean his teeth and guarantee him they'd stay white, because this Maria had put a curse on him and made them turn black. So that was my introduction to my new brother-in-law. He's telling there's a curse on his teeth."

Nau remained on the farm for a year. "At first he seemed weird but not scary," Cissie says. "Then he became unpredictable. For example, he didn't want to spend money on dog food for his dog, so he took a calf that died and hacked it up."

He would also utter loud unprovoked screams, and crawl through bedroom windows in the middle of the night to frighten other family members. One night he gutted a cow that had died of natural causes and slept inside the carcass.

When his dog was run over and killed on the highway he buried it on the farm without telling anyone.

DeBecker phoned Delmar Nau about Ralph twice, and urged him to seek help for his son. "'I'm afraid he's another John Hinckley,'" Delmar told DeBecker, but he was unable to coax his son into treatment. The entire family feared him.

In January 1984, Nau announced that he was returning to Los Angeles. He asked for money. When Delmar refused, Nau pointed a rifle at him, precipitating what Delmar described as a "two hour stare-down." When Nau finally left the farm, his family was relieved.

Instead of going to Los Angeles, he flew to Australia again. In Sydney he became disoriented and somehow made his way to the outback where he wandered for weeks. The only clues to what he did there come from his letters. "I keep remembering I killed someone," he wrote Maria C/O Newton-John.

He was taken into custody for his own protection in a small town in the outback and released to the Red Cross in Sydney, where Delmar sent him a plane ticket. As soon as he arrived on the farm he wrote Newton-John, saying "I feel like the thing that has a gun to your head." A few days later he wrote of his plans to kill someone: "I'll take him out back, shoot him and bury him there."

I Hit Something with an Ax

Delmar and Shirley Nau were divorced around the time Ralph returned from Australia. Shirley married Ken Gerken Sr. and Ralph moved with her to the Gerken farm near Antioch, Illinois. Gerken had two children from his first marriage, Ken Jr., 26, and Dennis, eight. Dennis had been with his mother when she collapsed and died of a stroke six years earlier. He hadn't uttered a word since, and was considered autistic.

"He was just an angel," says Ken Jr. "If Denny liked you he wouldn't leave you alone, and he liked Ralph. It was hard to know how Ralph felt about him. He would never show emotion unless he was watching TV. Then he'd be jumping up and down and screaming, `Yeah, yeah!'" The Gerkens often left Denny in Nau's care when they left the farm.

By then he had a new obsession. The 1984 Olympics were coming up, and he wrote Newton-John: "I know I am to watch as much of the Olympics as possible." He would later tell psychiatrists he was receiving messages from the Romanian gymnastics squad.

On the evening of August eighth, Nau was watching the Olympics by himself in the living room. His mother, her new husband, and her parents were in the family room. Shirley asked Nau if he wanted some ice cream and he shouted, "No." A short time later Denny tugged at him, trying to get his attention. When Nau ordered him out of the room and slammed the door, Ken Gerken got mad and told Nau that Denny could go anywhere he wanted. Nau immersed himself in the television without responding. About 9:30, Shirley put Dennis to bed.

Shortly after ten o'clock Nau walked into the family room, looking "sweaty and disheveled" according to police reports.

"Denny was crying," he told the assembled family members, "and when I went to his room he wasn't there."

Gerken called the Lake County sheriff, and the family began to search for Dennis. Soon investigator Chester Iwan arrived at the farm. He interviewed Nau, who said he'd had a dream in which Denny's mother told him she wanted her son to join her in heaven. Fearing the worst, Iwan took Nau to the Lake County sheriff's office in Waukegan and questioned him. After listening to him babble for more than an hour ("I went to Australia to visit Olivia. Elton John was so kind as to pay my way home"), Iwan told him it was time to talk about Denny.

Nau stared at the floor and replied, "A couple weeks ago my dog was killed by a truck. I buried it, but the other day I opened up the egg cooler and the dog was there."

"Where had you buried it?" Iwan asked.

"By a tree in the cornfield," Nau replied.

Iwan radioed investigators on the farm to search for a grave near a tree in the cornfield. There they found the body of Dennis Gerken. His skull had been crushed by repeated blows with a heavy object. A pattern of blood indicated he had been dragged in a semicircle before he was buried.

The next morning, after 11 straight hours of questioning, Nau made what was characterized as a confession. "I hit something with an ax," he told police. "I went down to Denny's room and got him dressed, but when we got outside he wasn't human any more. . . . I got the ax by the feed bin, and the shovel was out by the hole. When we got by the tree the animal tried to get away and started crying, and I swung at it with the ax and hit it in the head. Then I dug a hole and buried the animal. Then I came back in the house, scrubbed my boots and washed my clothes, and went up and watched the Olympics. After this I checked Denny's room and saw he wasn't there, so I told the family Denny was gone."

As far as investigators were concerned, they had their man. They gathered what physical evidence there was, none of it worth much: the shovel, Nau's boots, and some fabric from the clothes he'd worn.

"I believe it was premeditated," says Ken Gerken, Jr. "Why? Because the whole incident couldn't have taken more than half an hour, from the time the family saw Denny last until Ralph said he was missing, and it was probably a mile round trip. He had to walk a half mile to the back yard, dig a hole, kill him, bury him, put the shovel in the top of a feed hopper, and go downstairs and change his clothes. It's just not possible, unless the grave was already dug."

Ken Gerken, Jr., harbors surprisingly little malice toward Nau. "He's sick. How can you hate him?" he asks. "Maybe he really wanted Denny to be with his mom."

Randall Stewart was an assistant state's attorney in Lake County in 1984. "I was assigned the prosecution of Mr. Nau for the murder of his stepbrother," he says. "When I got the case, he'd made what I viewed as a valid confession. The court ordered an examination to determine whether he was capable of understanding the charges against him and was able to assist in his own defense. Those are the guidelines in Illinois law. The doctors found him unfit, so he was remanded to the state facility for treatment."

Months of drug and other therapy followed, but his condition didn't improve, and he was never deemed fit. "Under those circumstances," Stewart says, "a person has the right to require the state to prove him guilty beyond a reasonable doubt in order to continue holding him. The logic is undeniable. The state shouldn't be able to just yank you off the street, find you unfit for trial then let you rot in an institution even though they can't prove your guilt."

A hearing was scheduled on whether Nau had, beyond a reasonable doubt, killed his young stepbrother. But first Lake County public defender David Brodsky, who represented Nau, petitioned to have his confession thrown out, saying that, because of his mental condition, Nau was unable to understand his rights, and that police had played upon his inability to distinguish reality from fantasy. The court agreed. Nau's statement was deemed inadmissible.

The subsequent murder hearing took place before a single judge in May 1989. The prosecution's burden was the same as it would have been in a jury trial: prove Nau guilty beyond a reasonable doubt.

"As a man who's been on both sides of the fence," Stewart says, "I think the process is unfair. If he is found innocent he walks. But if the judge decides that the preponderance of evidence suggests guilt, the verdict has no criminal court standing. It means only that the state mental health department can hold him until he's found fit for trial, at which point he's given a full jury trial. In the meantime, of course, the prosecution had to show all its evidence at the first hearing, and expose its witnesses to cross-examination. It's a kind of double jeopardy reversed."

In Nau's case, the prosecution lost. Judge Stephen Walter initially found Nau guilty, but after reflecting on the matter overnight, he reversed himself. He explained in court that although he felt Nau had probably committed the murder, such a finding would almost certainly be overturned by a higher court because of the lack of corroborating physical evidence.

Nau's defense lawyers viewed the verdict as a vindication. "Who killed Dennis Gerken? Nobody will ever know," says John Greenlees, a Lake County public defender who worked on Nau's case. "There is no way Ralph could have done what they said he did in the time frame they claim it happened. It's just not possible. That is why the judge found him not guilty at the discharge hearing. There was no physical evidence; the time sequence just did not work; and the confession, if you can call it that, had been thrown out."

The prosecution responded by filing an immediate petition for Nau's civil commitment as a danger to himself and others. "I really thought it was absurd to say he could just walk out the door," Stewart says. "A different judge agreed and said the evidence, including the confession, which was admissible in a civil proceeding, showed that he was a danger."

Nau was sent to the Elgin Mental Health Center as an involuntary admission on May 31, 1989. A few days later Stewart took it upon himself to send a letter to a list of 40 stars that Nau was fixated upon, including Newton-John, newscaster Connie Chung, Farrah Fawcett, and Madonna. The prosecutor referred to Nau's bizarre behavior and his demonstrated ability to get near the objects of his delusional attachments. "We feel his release is imminent," wrote Stewart, "and we strongly feel he is a potential threat to you. We suggest you contact the Elgin mental-health facility regarding his release and intended whereabouts."

Stewart still feels as strongly as ever about Ralph Nau. "He can't help himself," he says. "He is a very frightening guy. But he was able to function. And he was in Los Angeles for a purpose, to get near the stars. He is violent. He is a very dangerous man."

Nau's condition has not improved since he was committed. A psychiatric report states: "Mr. Nau's delusional content is ingrained and untouchable. He is firmly convinced that many famous ladies in the TV are communicating with him, are in love with him, and anxiously await his release."

In 1990, he was transferred from the Elgin facility because of fears he might escape and make his way to Chicago to try to find a Chicago newscaster who had become his latest obsession. She was relieved when he was moved to downstate Chester, not only because he was in a more secure setting, but because he was out of television range.

"It's been better since they moved him," she says. "I don't have to think about him staring at me while I'm on camera."

Nau is eligible to petition for release every six months. The standard by which his petitions are measured is this: Has he advanced toward his therapeutic goals? Has he, in other words, learned to control and overcome his erotomania? Or is he likely to be a threat to himself or others if he's released?

Timothy O'Neil, the former Kane County state's attorney who opposed Nau's first petition for release in 1990, thinks there is a good chance someday he will be able to convince the release board that he has gotten better, that he's not a threat.

"For all his mental illness, he is very creative and crafty," O'Neil says. Like Stewart and other court officers who have dealt with Nau, O'Neil thinks it's a pity the system has no provision to ensure Nau's continued confinement. "At his release hearings, he argues that he never explicitly threatens anyone. But imagine what would happen if he did get out. He'd go find whoever his current obsession is, but what will happen when he is rejected? He's going to get killed himself by some star's security guard, or he's going to harm someone. He belongs in custody, very secure custody."

"Sooner or later he'll get out," says Ken Gerken, Jr. "We're sure of that, and I'm sure he could do this kind of thing again."

As for Nau, when he is not discussing his relationships with celebrities, he can be surprisingly lucid. In a July 1991 letter concerning this article, he wrote: "I can't stop you reporters from printing bad stuff about me. All I can tell you is that I never threatened anyone. If you want to print something just put down for me that I'm a sweetheart kind of a guy."

Ralph Nau remains in custody in the Illinois mental health system.

The Key Man

The Key Man

Early one morning in May 1973, somebody knocked on the back door of the B & B wholesale florist shop on E. Hennepin Avenue in Minneapolis. The owner, Robert Nachtscheim, hadn't opened yet but he let the caller in anyway, so it was probably someone he knew. If he thought it was a friend he was wrong. The mysterious caller killed him with a shotgun blast to the head.

No one has ever been indicted for Nachtscheim's murder, but the family dynamics surrounding the crime are as convoluted and emotionally charged as a Greek tragedy, and so much cash changed hands because of it that the killing became a virtual industry—a kind of Murder Inc.

For ten years before he opened his own business in 1972, Nachtscheim sold flowers for another wholesaler, Midwest Florist Supply Company.

"Bob was a great flower salesman," says his widow, Betty. "He knew the trade inside and out. He didn't just sell flowers to his accounts. He practically ran their businesses for some of them. They relied on him for everything."

Betty worked at Midwest along with her husband. It would later be claimed that she was given a clerical job to keep her super-salesman husband in the fold. That certainly factored into the decision, but there were other good reasons to hire her. She was a competent enough employee, and such a stunning-looking woman that men who owned flower shops chose to do business with Midwest just to spend a few minutes in her presence.

Midwest also employed the Nachtscheims' son, Bobby Jr., 21. People dropped around to see Bobby too, but they weren't looking for flowers, they were looking for buds off the cannabis bush. Norm Wartnick, part-owner and manager of Midwest, suspected that Bobby earned most of his income accommodating them, but he was hesitant to fire him because his dad kept the business afloat.

Robert Nachtscheim Sr. was never paid more than $260 a week, but his employers thought so highly of his abilities that they took out a "key man" insurance policy in the amount of $100,000, payable to the firm, in case he died.

In August 1972, Nachtscheim decided to strike out on his own. He and Betty talked about the terms of his departure with Wartnick. They told him to drop the key man policy, and threatened to sue if he didn't. Betty later called the agent who'd written the insurance, Zola Friedman, and reiterated their demands. Friedman told her he had no power to make Midwest cancel the policy, but he doubted they would keep it now that their employee had left.

Nachtscheim took 90 percent of Midwest's business with him when he departed, leaving the company in desperate straits. It had few assets, but it had a liability that could turn into an asset under the right circumstances. The annual premium on the key man policy, due in April 1973, was $2650. Interest payable to the policy holder could be applied against that sum, leaving a total of $1050 due. It was a lot of money for a failing business to pay, and Midwest no longer had an insurable interest in its' former employee's life. Nevertheless, on May 13, 1973, at the end of a 31 day grace period, the policy was renewed.

Less than two weeks later Nachtscheim was murdered.

****

Detective William Quinn of the Minneapolis police was the first investigator on the scene. "I always thought it was a planned murder, not a robbery," Quinn says. "Nothing was missing from the shop, and the victim's wallet with about $300 in it was in plain sight where he fell."

So was a box of orchids that Nachtscheim had apparently taken out of the cooler moments before he was shot.

"That was a wholesale quantity of orchids," says Betty Nachtscheim, "and I told the investigators what it meant. Another florist had gained entrance on the pretense that he wanted to buy flowers from Bob. Florists often accommodate each other that way."

Betty had a specific florist in mind. She still does. "I have always believed that it was Norm Wartnick who killed Bob," she says. "We were interested in ending the hard feelings that existed between Norm and us because Bob had quit. If Norm had come to the door, Bob would have let him in."

Investigator Quinn was soon joined at the scene by a second detective, Russell Krueger. The two agreed that Krueger would lead the investigation. Krueger had a long and colorful career in law enforcement, dating back to a time when, in his words, "our size 12 shoe was the only search warrant we needed."

A beefy, pugnacious man, Krueger started out as a vice cop in the 1950s. After several years trapping prostitutes and gays, he made detective in 1957. His career languished at that point, because the criminals he found himself dealing with, and often consorting with, didn't provoke the moral outrage he needed to get motivated. The 1960s were the best thing that ever happened to him in that respect. His single-minded efforts to rid Minneapolis of weed-smoking hippies garnered him reams of publicity, and a promotion to the homicide division. By the time Bob Nachtscheim was murdered he'd investigated more than 300 homicides. A video-taped interrogation he conducted was used on a TV cop show as a case study in how to violate a suspect's rights.

Krueger was a throwback to another era in law enforcement, but even his critics—and he had many, both in and out of the department—had to admit that he was an effective investigator. Nevertheless, it was slow going on the Nachtscheim case. There was no hard evidence to be found, but plenty of conflicting information.

The evening of the murder, Betty Nachtscheim called Krueger and told him about the key man life insurance policy. She fingered Norm Wartnick.

The victim's father had other ideas. He banged Krueger's ear with tales of Betty Nachtscheim's alleged infidelities, and of the animosity that Bob's daughter Angie felt toward her dad. He was sure that someone in the family was responsible for his son's death.

Neither party had anything but their certainties to offer, however. And there was nothing at the scene to connect anyone to the crime. There were a few clues—the key man policy, the box of orchids, and the fact that Nachtscheim was killed with a load of birdshot fired at extremely close range. The blast wouldn't have been fatal at more than a few feet because of the nature of the ammunition. That clashed with the theory that it was a planned murder; a hand gun would have been more effective, and far easier to conceal. Was it a bungled attempt at robbery? The possibility couldn't be discounted.

Early in the investigation Krueger and Betty Nachtscheim began to socialize at the Blue Ox Lounge in downtown Minneapolis, where Krueger worked as a part-time bouncer. Betty's daughter, Teri Peters, often went along to keep an eye on her mom.

"To tell you the truth I was worried about her," says Peters, "not only because she was drinking too much for the first time in her life, but because I didn't like the scene there. I especially didn't like Russ Krueger's behavior. I remember him getting into a drunken argument with some people once, and waving a loaded pistol around while he was shouting at them. I was thinking, this guy is a cop. He could shoot somebody and get away with it. Russ was a scary guy. He sure scared me."

Peters was surprised to hear that Krueger was working at the Blue Ox when he and her mother were there. "I always thought he just hung out and drank," she says. "That was how it looked."

In the 1970s, off-duty Minneapolis cops were allowed to work at bars. It was later forbidden (now it's okay again), for a variety of reasons, including the one that Peters observed. The combination of alcohol and guns was considered too volatile, instances of police officers enforcing bar rules as if they were the laws that they were sworn to uphold had become common and there were some bars where a cop/bouncer was bound to rub shoulders with criminals.

According to Betty, she and Krueger socialized with gangsters at the Blue Ox, among them the late Ferris Alexander, the Minneapolis-based pornography kingpin. Alexander did a stretch in a federal penitentiary in the 1980s for pornography-related charges. The feds characterized him as an important organized crime figure. He and Russ were pals, and Russ also got along well with Louie Rittaco, a mafia-connected burglar, Jerry Conaway, another master burglar, and Bob Marshallton, self-styled "gemologist" and fence.

Peters wasn't happy about her mother's involvement with Krueger, but she understood what prompted it. "Mom wanted to keep him interested in the case. She wanted to make sure he stayed on top of it, and checked out any information we came across. And he'd tell her things about the investigation. I can still hear her saying, 'I've got to go meet Russ because he's going to tell me something about dad.'"

Wartnick has a different view. "Betty Nachtscheim was a beautiful woman, and Russ Krueger was a big sweaty clunk," he says. "Did she have some attraction to him? I doubt it." He believes Betty's relationship with Krueger allowed her to skew the investigation toward him, and away from her family. Both Betty and Krueger admit to a sexual relationship, a one night stand that occurred during the investigation. Krueger, a born-again Christian, has since told Wartnick's attorneys that in his opinion the affair was immoral, but not unethical.

Inspector Sherman Otto, who was Commander of Criminal Investigations for the Minneapolis Police in the early 1990s, when the case got a second look, disagrees. "It was improper, and it was unethical," Otto says.

Betty regrets her affair with Krueger, but denies any hidden agendas. "I didn't have ulterior motives of any kind with Russ," she says. "I was drinking then, I was unhappy and vulnerable, desperate really, and he was around. That's all." Queried whether Krueger may have had some loyalties to her that compromised his investigation, she laughs. "He had loyalties alright, but not to me or my family."

She believes Krueger was less than thorough because he was protecting Ferris Alexander. "Ferris was laundering money through Midwest while Bob worked there," she says. "I think Ferris put Norm up to killing my husband to save the business. Midwest was important to him."

Its' importance, she claims, was based on a quirk of the flower industry. Poets have observed that the beauty of a rose is most exquisite just before it starts to wither. Street people have noticed the same thing, and hustlers peddling moribund roses have been familiar figures in bars and clubs around the Twin Cities for decades. They go to wholesale florists, buy a few dozen roses that were destined for the trash bin for next to nothing, sell them for a dollar a bloom, and pocket the difference.

According to Betty, Ferris Alexander organized that trade, enabling him to wash bundles of money by putting hundreds of peddlers in bars and on street corners every weekend. She claims it was a good deal for Midwest. It allowed them to err on the long side when they ordered, knowing they'd never get stuck with large quantities of blooms that had become worthless.

"I guess it's possible that Ferris bankrolled flower peddlers, I don't know" says attorney Randall Tigue, who defended Alexander in court many times. "I dealt exclusively with the free speech issues raised by the pornography charges he faced. He did begin his business career with a flower shop in downtown Minneapolis."

But Betty was unable to explain why Alexander's connection with Midwest was worth killing to protect. Wholesale florists refer to the street people who pester them for stale roses as "nuts," but they tolerate them, and even extend them credit, because it enables the florists to milk a few last dollars out of their inventory. Midwest wasn't the only wholesaler that would welcome someone who could organize that business, and pay cash in front. Ferris Alexander faced many pornography-related charges in his life but he was never accused of murder, and it wasn't for lack of investigators probing his affairs. Besides, there were far better suspects, most notably Norm Wartnick.

Soon after the murder, Wartnick hired attorney Phil Gainsley to represent him in two matters—the payment of the insurance money, and the investigation itself. Wartnick contacted Gainsley shortly after Russ Krueger stopped by his home for a chat.

Wartnick presented his alibi, which was shaky. He said he'd slept in the spare bedroom the night before Nachtscheim was killed, because his wife was having a card party and he didn't want to be disturbed when she came to bed late. Therefore, no one could verify that he'd been home about 6 A.M., when the murder occurred.

Queried why he renewed the key man policy, Wartnick claimed he'd intended it as an enticement to persuade Nachtscheim to return to Midwest. He said he planned to offer Nachtscheim the dividends as a yearly bonus, and to promise him the full cash value when he reached age 65.

"During the questioning of Mr. Wartnick he was visibly shaken, his body was trembling," wrote Krueger in his report. "He would become noticeably more upset when I would bring up the $100,000 policy."

A few days later Krueger interviewed Zola Friedman, the Prudential agent who wrote the policy. He asked Friedman why Midwest could get insurance on someone who didn't work for them. Because Nachtscheim agreed to be insured when the policy was written, Friedman explained, and since it had never lapsed, no further permission was necessary.

According to Friedman, when he heard Nachtscheim had quit Midwest he reacted in true insurance agent's fashion, by attempting to sell Nachtscheim a key man policy on himself for his new business. Nachtscheim was cool to the idea, and Friedman admitted that during the conversation Nachtscheim threatened to sue Prudential if the company didn't cancel Midwest's policy.

Krueger hammered away at the contradiction inherent in insuring someone's life against their will. Isn't it a little strange, he said, that Norm Wartnick paid that premium with just one day left until it would be canceled, and just 13 days later the insured party is found shot in the head with a shotgun?

Friedman said he was sorry about that because he considered Bob a friend, but neither he nor the company had anything to do with his murder.

"All during the questioning the man would mop his brow and wring his hands," Krueger wrote in his report. He said this indicated that Friedman wanted to get something off his chest. Others have observed that wringing of the hands and mopping of the brow, not to mention peeing of the pants, are natural human reactions to an interrogation by Russ Krueger. When the detective told Friedman that Wartnick had likewise been nervous when he was questioned, Friedman replied, "Good God, I can believe it. Who wouldn't be?"

In December 1973, attorney Gainsley wrote his client Norm Wartnick a letter in which he reiterated his belief that a suit he was about to file at Wartnick's behest was ill-advised. It begins: "As you know, we have refrained from commencing an action against Prudential for the recovery of benefits resulting from the death of Robert T. Nachtscheim because we have been advised that you are a suspect in the death of Mr. Nachtscheim."

The letter put Wartnick's denial of guilt on the record, as well as some details about Midwest's financial situation, which was grim. It described the possible consequences of filing for recovery—legal hassles, multiple depositions, adverse publicity, plus "embarrassment and humiliation," but concluded by stating that as soon as the other shareholders in Midwest acknowledged reading and understanding a copy of the letter, Gainsley would commence the recovery action per Wartnick's request.

One year later, after receiving assurances from Hennepin County Attorney Gary Flakne that no charges would be filed, Prudential paid up.

* * *

Wartnick was an obvious suspect, but he wasn't the only one. Bob Nachtscheim Sr. was notorious for his extra-marital affairs, many of which involved women he dropped by to service at florist shops where they worked. Could an angry husband or a jilted lover have killed him? The way his face had been massacred by the shotgun blast suggested that, but nothing specific ever surfaced and more promising leads did.

During his investigation Krueger became aware of a party that had taken place at the home of Bobby Nachtscheim Jr. and his girlfriend Debby Feist the night before Bobby Sr. was murdered. Accounts of what occurred there raised questions.

Bobby Jr. was interviewed soon after the murder. He told Krueger he'd left his employment at Midwest at the same time his father did, in order to work with him at B & B. Bobby Jr. said he and Bobby Sr. had parted ways that past January, after arguing constantly, not only about the business, but about his break-up with a young woman from Mound, Minnesota, whom his father liked, and his relationship with Debbie Feist, who his father didn't like. Bobby claimed his father had called him the afternoon before the murder and asked him to return to work, but he'd refused.

Then they discussed the party. Bobby initially said he'd been drinking until the early morning hours, but soon amended that to say he'd fallen asleep shortly after midnight. He told Krueger that he'd found out about his father's murder when he awoke the next morning.

Debbie Feist confirmed his story. She said Bobby went to bed around midnight, about the time the other guests were leaving. She'd gone out for pizza, and returned about 1:30 to find Bobby still asleep. They were both awakened at 7:30 the following morning by a phone call informing them of the murder.

Over the next few days more details about the party were revealed. Among the guests was Dennis Kreuser, 20, a former B & B employee. He'd been paroled from St. Cloud prison, where he was serving time for robbery, six months before the murder. Bobby's sister Angie had arranged for her father to hire Kreuser after she became his pen pal and discovered that his release was contingent on employment. Kreuser and Angie started going together shortly after his release.

According to Betty Nachtscheim, her husband had fired Kreuser in March 1973, because of his poor work habits. She said Kreuser had come around B & B a few weeks before the murder and attempted to sell Nachtscheim Sr. some merchandise that he assumed was stolen.

"Bob told him to get out and stay out," says Betty.

Kreuser disputed that account. He claimed he'd lost the job because of his relationship with Angie, which infuriated Betty. He said he'd overheard Betty demanding that her husband give him five days' notice, so he tendered his resignation instead.

Angie had accepted an engagement ring from Kreuser at Christmas time, but they were miffed at each other the night of Bobby Jr.'s party. Angie was one of the guests, but she spent much of her time with another young man, Larry Strehlow. Like several others at the party, drink brought out the worst in Strehlow. That evening he simply went home, he claimed, but that wasn't his usual M O. He was in the curious habit of going to cemeteries and tipping over gravestones when he was loaded, a pastime that cost him dearly a short while later.

Roger Nordstrom also attended the bash at Bobby and Debbie's place. He was a high school friend of Bobby's, a gun collector and a drug dealer, who'd once lived with Bobby, and had a run-in with Bobby's parents. Bobby Sr. had loaned his son some money to buy a car. Bobby got so far behind on the payments that his father announced he was coming to take the automobile. According to Betty, when they arrived Nordstrom was standing on the porch with a shotgun.

"He threatened to kill my husband if he took the car," Betty told Krueger.

According to her, they went to the Roseville Police, got a police escort, and took the car anyway. Both Nordstrom and Bobby deny it ever happened (Nordstrom flatly denied it, Bobby said he "couldn't recall" it), but the investigators found a record of the incident in the Roseville Police Department's files.

Shortly after Nachtscheim was murdered, Nordstrom left the Twin Cities area permanently.

Kreuser, Strehlow, and Bobby Jr. were each questioned several times by different investigators, who discovered that cocaine, pot and beer were all consumed at the party, and the possibility of robbing Bob Nachtscheim Sr. had come up in conversation. Bobby characterized the talk as "just a bunch of guys shooting the bull." He claims that he told the others it would be easy to get money from his father, because he always hung his pants on a hook in the bathroom before he went to bed, and left his wallet, which routinely contained up to $500 cash, in his pocket. Bobby said he suggested opening the bathroom window, which was never locked, and using a long pole to snag the pants.

More than a year later Dennis Kreuser told Russ Krueger that it was actually an armed robbery of B & B Florists that was discussed at the party, and Bobby had done most of the talking. Kreuser's information was suspect however, because he was in federal prison when he provided it, and Bobby helped put him there. Bobby had sent a friend of his to buy drugs from Kreuser, at Russ Krueger's bidding.

Why Krueger and Bobby Jr. conspired to trap Kreuser is a mystery. Was it a genuine effort to solve the murder of Bobby Sr. by putting pressure on a key witness? Was it a way to take a key witness out of circulation before he got someone into trouble? Or was it a clever plot to put a weak link in a position in which any information he offered was nullified? The fact that the latter possibilities can't be discounted illustrates something fundamental about law enforcement. Faulty police work opens the door to all kinds of speculation. Some of it is bound to make the innocent look guilty, and vice versa.

The truth about Kreuser's entrapment may lie in the investigation files, but they are closed because there is no statute of limitations on murder, so technically they concern an active case. In reality the case is cold as death, for several reasons. Decades have passed, so has at least one important figure, and most crucially, key portions of the file are missing. Neither Krueger nor Inspector Otto can explain how they disappeared, but Krueger admits that he kept the files when he left the police department to go to work for the Hennepin County Public Defender's office. He is now retired.

"It was the only homicide case I ever investigated that wasn't brought to court, and it bothered me," Krueger said, "so I took the file." He made that admission in a deposition taken for a civil case stemming from the murder. He claimed he'd referred to the file when he made inquiries of his own down through the years.

If that's true, then his zeal after the county attorney decided not to charge the case contrasts sharply with his approach when aggressive police work might have led to an arrest. He claimed his investigation was stymied because he could never could interview the man he characterized as "the missing link," Roger Nordstrom. He said he made the rounds of Nordstrom's hangouts and questioned a variety of people about where he'd gone, but came up with nothing for a long time. When he finally discovered Nordstrom had moved to Austin, Texas, Krueger claims he asked for plane fare from Captain Carl Johnson, who headed homicide, but was refused.

"That doesn't sound right on the face of it," says Inspector Otto.

Krueger also claims he called an investigator he knew in the Austin police department and asked him to find Nordstrom, but "the missing link" couldn't be located. That doesn't sound right either, because a private investigator who was hired in connection with one of the subsequent civil cases found Nordstrom easily.

That investigator deposed Nordstrom in Austin, where he'd been living, and making no efforts to conceal himself. He had a listed phone number under his own name. Nordstrom denied any involvement in Nachtscheim's murder, and said there were several Twin Citians who'd known his where-abouts but hadn't been asked.

Any efforts Krueger might have made to get information from Larry Strehlow were frustrated as well. Not long after the murder Strehlow was found crushed under a gravestone that weighed almost two tons. The police who investigated his death concluded that he'd somehow managed to tip the stone over on himself. The fact that the spot where he died was just a few yards from Robert Nachtscheim's grave, they decided, was mere coincidence.

Wartnick and others have speculated that Strehlow's flat-tened corpse and its position near Nachtscheim's grave may have been a message to those with knowledge about the killing.

When Dennis Kreuser was questioned in prison in 1975, he explained that he'd lied to protect Bobby two years earlier because he considered him a friend at the time. He was willing to offer the truth now, he told Krueger, because his ex-pal had busted him.

He told Krueger that Bobby was not asleep when the party broke up, as he'd previously stated. He said Bobby, Feist, and Roger Nordstrom left together about one o'clock a.m. Kreuser said he'd asked Bobby what happened after he heard about the shooting, and Bobby simply replied that he was now part owner of a wholesale flower business.

He also claimed that Bobby had canceled plans to marry the young woman from Mound, Minnesota. and married Debbie Feist so she could never testify against him. He told Krueger that when he asked Bobby about his marriage to Feist, Bobby just smiled.

Kreuser's information was intriguing, but it was offered under circumstances that rendered it useless to a prosecutor. Those circumstances were cooked up by two people—the lead investigator, who'd been thoroughly corrupted, and the suspect that the information concerned. When Kreuser talked he was serving his second stretch in a penitentiary. He admitted he'd lied previously, and said he was offering the revised account to even a score.

It was either an unfortunate or serendipitous turn of events, depending on one's point of view.

* * *

Robert Nachtscheim Sr. wasn't paid what he was worth when he was alive, but he made plenty of money for other people. Maybe he stiffed someone in a former life. If so, his karmic debt must have been outstanding when he died. Once the authorities gave up on solving his murder he resumed his old role.

The first payment prompted by his death was $100,000—the proceeds of the key man insurance policy that went to his former employers, Midwest Florists. That company had lived off his efforts for years, but his posthumous contribution wasn't enough to keep it afloat. It soon went out of business.

Prudential's decision to pay on the policy stuck in Betty Nachtscheim's craw. In November 1974 she retained attorney Ron Meshbesher. The two of them began to explore the possibility of lawsuits against the insurer and or Wartnick.

"It was an intriguing case," says Meshsbesher, "but difficult from the evidentiary standpoint. We had motive but nothing else. I thought it was very upsetting that a company could issue a policy on someone's life, then let the policy be taken out of the insured party's control. When Nachtscheim left Wartnick's employ, both Mr. And Mrs. Nachtscheim told the agent they wanted the policy canceled, but there was no way to force Wartnick to cancel it. That's damned strange. It actually creates an incentive."

Meshbesher sat on the lawsuit in hopes that additional evidence would surface. Occasionally he made inquiries of the police, but he discovered that things were worse than he thought. There was some chance that if anything did surface it would incriminate his client's son, not Norm Wartnick. But Betty remained convinced that Wartnick was the killer. She urged him to act.

Almost two years after she retained him, a reluctant Meshbesher filed an unjust enrichment claim against Prudential, Midwest, and Wartnick. It was a claim that he admits smacked of wrongful death allegations, because it was based on Nachtscheim's murder.

Why wasn't the suit actually for wrongful death?

"Well, that's an embarrassment to me," says Meshbesher, "Somehow our tickler system went awry, and the statute of limitations on wrongful death ran out."

He explains that the unjust enrichment claim was questionable. "My case would have been based on the proposition that Wartnick acted against the public interest in renewing the insurance, and therefore should not have been allowed to benefit. If he couldn't pay, then I'd have said the insurer should. Could we have won? Well, never say never, but I'm glad I didn't have to make that argument."

The reason he didn't involves some legal twists that are just as tangled as the criminal aspects of the case. During the pre-trial maneuvering, which took years, Gainsley brought Wartnick in for a deposition by Meshbesher. According to Wartnick, his attorney didn't advise him how to handle the questioning until the last moment, and then the advice was cursory.

"He just handed me a card, and told me to read off it in answer to every question unless he specifically instructed me to do otherwise," says Wartnick. "The card read, 'I respectfully decline to answer that question on grounds that it may violate my rights under the Fifth Amendment of the Constitution.'"

Predictably, Meshbesher asked Wartnick if he'd killed Nachtscheim, or hired anyone else to do so. In reply, he took the Fifth.

"I was pleasantly surprised to say the least," says Meshbesher. "He had already given a statement to the police, so it wasn't as if he was maintaining silence. It was a big mistake in my opinion. In Minnesota the fact finder in a civil case is allowed to draw an adverse inference when someone takes the Fifth. Without that we'd have never gotten to a jury. The judge said as much in one of his orders. Until then the law was all on Wartnick's side. He owned the policy, he'd paid the premiums, and he had a right to collect."

Years later Gainsley would contend that answering the question would have opened Wartnick to a withering cross examination by Meshbesher, a premiere trial attorney and former prosecutor. According to Gainsley, something Wartnick said could have put him in jeopardy of criminal charges.

In light of the new development, Meshbesher began kicking himself all the harder for missing the wrongful death deadline. He asked his clerk to research whether there was any way to remedy his error within the law as written. The answer was no.

Gainsley gave his clerk a task as well. He wrote him a memo saying he'd instructed his client to take the Fifth, then had been told by Meshbesher that the jury could draw an adverse inference. "How does taking the Fifth affect civil liability?' was his question to the clerk. "Obviously," he added, "I would like your answer to be it does not."

His clerk, an associate who hoped to make partner, was glad to accommodate. He wrote a report concluding that liability was not affected by taking the Fifth. Gainsley took him at his word. It would turn out to be a grievous error, because Meshbesher was right, not the clerk.

Gainsley had a long time to remedy his error. The case didn't come to trial for years. But he made no effort to put Wartnick on record denying the crime.

In 1977, Prudential settled out of court with Betty Nachtscheim for $75,000 and was severed from the case. Meshbesher began lobbying the state legislature for a change in the wrongful death statute.

"I pointed out a discrepancy," he says. "There is no statute of limitations on criminal cases involving murder, but there was a limitation in civil cases. I portrayed changing that as victim's rights legislation, which it is in my opinion."

The bill that did away with the civil limitation was drafted in Meshbesher's office, and written to be retroactive. It became law in 1983. Betty Nachtscheim's complaint was immediately amended to include wrongful death.

The case finally went to trial in 1986. In Meshbesher's opinion, Gainsley made another error when he allowed his client to answer queries about the deposition from the stand, rather than having a clerk simply read it verbatim. Thus, Meshbesher was able to repeat his earlier query, then ask Wartnick if he'd taken the Fifth in reply.

"Did I ask you whether you killed Robert Nachtscheim or hired someone to do so?" he asked.

"Yes," said Wartnick.

"And did you reply that you declined to answer on grounds that it would violate your Fifth Amendment protection against self-incrimination?"

"Yes," Wartnick said.

According to Meshbesher, that was the turning point of the trial. "You could hear the jurors catch their breath when it happened," he says.

Another moment of high drama came when Russ Krueger took the stand. "It's beyond comprehension," he testified, "that a man can get an insurance policy on another man and two weeks later he's shot in the head and killed." Then he rose from the stand and shouted—"AND THE ONLY MAN THAT BENEFITTED FROM IT WAS THAT MAN RIGHT THERE!" He pointed at Wartnick.

A few days later the jury awarded Betty Nachtscheim $2.4 million. It was Pyrrhic victory. By then Wartnick was supporting himself by refereeing kids' basketball games. The court garnisheed his checks, which barely chipped away at the interest.

In 1988, Wartnick sued his attorney Phil Gainsley for malpractice. He cited the disastrous advice to take the Fifth, the flawed trial strategy that required him to answer in his own voice when asked if he'd done so, and Gainsley's failure to conduct an adequate investigation into the crime so he could pose an alternative to the theory that his client killed Nachtscheim for the insurance.

Wartnick's attorneys in the malpractice case hired an investigator who quickly tracked down Roger Nordstrom in Texas. At trial they presented investigators' reports and depositions about the party at Bobby and Debby's place, and what was discussed there. Nordstrom denied any involvement in Nachtscheim's murder, but Wartnick's lawyers' ability to pose a counter explanation was instrumental in the jury's decision. In October 1994, they found in Wartnick's favor, and awarded him $4 million. Two years later, while an appeal was pending, Gainsley's firm settled with Wartnick for $3 million.

Wartnick felt at least partially vindicated, but financially it was another Pyrrhic victory. Shortly after the malpractice suit was filed, Betty Nachtscheim had been granted a judicial lien on the proceeds of any verdict or settlement. After Wartnick won he moved to have the lien vacated, but in April 1996 he abandoned the effort, and settled with Betty for $1.4 million, everything that was left of his judgment after attorney's fees and court costs.

Getting his denial of guilt on the record helped Wartnick overcome a state of depression that he feared was permanent. "I considered suicide many times," he says. "I did not kill Robert Nachtscheim. I want the world to know that."

In the 1980s, Betty and her daughter Teri Peters lobbied a bill through the state legislature that gives an employee the right to take over a key man policy.

In 1990-91, the Minneapolis police conducted a second investigation of Robert Nachtscheim's murder. They decided there wasn't enough evidence to charge anyone with the crime.

Last Train

Last Train

Buzz Potter was a hobo in his youth, and the romance of the rails never lost its grip on him. Like many former hobos who went on to lead more prosaic lives, the 59-year-old still occasionally hops a freight for the thrill of it. It's become more dangerous than it used to be, he acknowledges, but he doubts that hobos are to blame.

"A hobo is a working stiff who uses the rails as free transportation," Potter explains. "He's neat, he's clean, he has a $20 bill tucked in his boot, and he's on his way to someplace where he's heard there is work. He is not a tramp, who will work if he has to, or a bum, who won't work under any circumstances. He is an itinerant working man with his own code and lingo, who takes pride in having his own independent lifestyle."

Potter has been in the mining and marine construction businesses most of his adult life. He once owned a bar in

Brainerd, Minnesota. Now he lives in nearby Nisswa where he publishes a magazine called The Hobo Times, "America's Journal of Wanderlust."

Hobos, he explains, date back to the immediate post-Civil War years, when demobilized soldiers from both armies roamed the country in search of work. Adrift in an agrarian society, they carried hoes because they were most likely to earn money weeding fields. They became known as "hoe-boys," but as time passed and the nature of the work changed, so did their name.

Hobos, tramps, and bums had the rails to themselves for decades, but no longer. "Now it's kind of a yuppie thing to hop a freight," says detective Chuck Oliver of the Salt Lake City police. His department makes it a point to warn stockbrokers, salespeople, and other weekend riders not to wear top-of-the-line gear when they catch out. "There are guys who will kill you for a good pair of hiking boots," he says.

In July of 1995, Buzz Potter and a buddy whose hobo nickname is Adman (because he owns a Minneapolis advertising agency) hopped a freight and traveled to the west coast and back. During a layover in the yards in Whitefish, Montana, they encountered a railroad cop who warned them that a hobo had been murdered in the area recently. He showed them where it happened.

"The victim had been beaten down with an ax handle," Potter recalls. "Then the perp picked up a steel fence post that was laying around with a clump of concrete still attached, and used that to smash the poor guy's head into the ground. Sawdust had been thrown around to cover the gore, but there were places they'd missed."

According to police, the crushed remains of the victim's head had been fastidiously covered with a portion of his shirt, as if the killer had meant to spare whoever discovered it the sight he'd left.

The rest of the trip was pleasant enough, and Potter repeated it the next year. "It'll take more than the fear of some nut to keep me off the rails," he says.

* * *

By 1995 there were six murders of transients under investigation in five states, including the one in Whitefish. Many more were unsolved but no longer on active status. Late that year, two more corpses were added to the list. The first one rolled into Millersburg, Oregon, in an open boxcar on December 3. The victim had been bludgeoned to death. What was left of his head was covered. He was identified as William Pettit, 39.

By tracking the boxcar's serial number against computerized route information, local police were able to conclude that Pettit had been murdered 20 miles to the north, in the yards at Salem, Oregon. Jurisdiction passed to the Salem police and the investigation was assigned to detective Mike Quakenbush.

"It's a frustrating kind of case," says Quakenbush. "There didn't seem to be anywhere to start. There were no witnesses. Pettit's relatives hadn't seen him for years. Was it random? Revenge? Robbery? You have no idea."

On December 6, another drifter, later identified as Michael Clites, 24, was found in a boxcar in Portland, clubbed to death with his crushed head covered. Because of the similarities between the two homicides, Quakenbush teamed up with a Portland detective. They started poking around in the transient community.

"I was pretty naive at the time," says Quakenbush. "I didn't know people rode the trains to the extent they do or that they all had nicknames. I'd never heard of this gang, the FTRA." He consulted with Spokane, Washington, investigator Robert Grandinetti.

Grandinetti's involvement with transients dates to 1982, when he was in charge of keeping downtown Spokane free of panhandlers. He noticed that many of the transients he hassled wore bandannas held together at the throat by a concho, a cowboy's saddle ring. The bandannas were mostly black, with a scattering of blue and red ones. They identified the wearers as members of the FTRA, Grandinetti was told. "The initials stood for Freedom Riders of America, or Freight Train Riders of America. I began to recognize their graffiti, which you will almost always see on railway underpasses and bridges."

The colors of the bandannas reflect three distinct FTRA factions, Grandinetti learned. Those who wear red mainly ride the rails across the southern U.S. Blue means they stick to the old Frisco line across the country's mid-section, and black belongs to riders of the so-called high line that runs from the Twin Cities to the state of Washington. Many FTRA members are Vietnam vets and ex-bikers, and many, Grandinetti says, espouse a racist ideology akin to that of the Aryan Nation.

In the mid-80s, while Grandinetti was learning about the FTRA, the bodies of eight transient men were found along the high line between Sand Point, Idaho, and Pasco, Washington. Their pants were down around their ankles, and their shirts had been pulled over their heads. Each was missing a limb.

"The authorities kind of dismissed it as railroad accidents," says Grandinetti, "but I don't buy it. One maybe, but eight?" The fact that each victim's clothes were positioned the same way struck him as a signature. The crimes were never solved.

Police and railroad detectives across the country have encountered other murder victims with their pants pulled down. Some have come to think of that as the calling card of the FTRA, which they characterize as a racist gang with its own grisly rituals and agenda, which includes murdering informers.

Grandinetti says FTRA members spoke readily to him about gang lingo, rituals, and petty crime, in general terms. They never provided information about specific criminal acts. Their usual MO was to take advantage of lax food stamp and welfare procedures by setting up recipient accounts in several states, often using stolen ID, then moving from place to place by rail to collect. They had a network of liquor and grocery stores at which they could turn food stamps to cash. One FTRA member could be using as many as six aliases in three or four states.

"They'll talk about what they do but they won't squeal," Grandinetti says. "Squealers are dealt with severely."

The black-bandana-clad high-liners, Grandinetti claims, are the most violent of the FTRA. A faction known as the Death Squad, he says, enforces the gang's agenda, which ranges from acquiring extra ID by committing murder, to taking revenge on squealers.

A sometimes resident of St. Paul called Tex claims to be acquainted with several FTRA members, including Dog-Man Tony, whom Grandinetti calls the head of the Death Squad.

"I talked to Dog-Man just the other day," says Tex. "He's down in La Crosse now. I rode with him and Sidetrack out in California, and look here, old Tuck, he wrote his name on my jacket. I got nothing bad to say about the FTRA, leastways not the older guys. Some of these younger ones who claim to be ragged and tagged FTRA, they're nothin' but wannabes. They're causing all the trouble.

"I started riding the rails in 1984," says Tex. He spends his days at the Dorothy Day Center in downtown St. Paul and nights at a camp along the railroad tracks near Lowertown, with a bottle of something to keep off the chill. "I was 20 years of age and fresh out of the penitentiary when I met some of these older guys, like Fast Cat and Half-Step. They asked me how come I was hitchhiking. Cuz I need a ride, I told 'em, and they said, 'then ride the rails with us, partner.'"

So he did, and he's been hopping freights ever since. He's been around St. Paul for the past two years, but he talks about catching out for Oklahoma. Not before taking certain precautions, though. You'd think someone like Tex, who is about the size of an NFL tight end, doesn't have much to be afraid of, but he says discretion is the better part of valor on the tracks these days.

"I'm gonna get me a pistol," he says. "Hell, I've got no choice. Ain't nobody gonna take my shit off me. That's what they're doing out there now. A lot of the guys I used to know retired because of it. They got addresses and everything."

Homeless kids who kill for kicks, or to make a name for themselves, are responsible for most of the violence in Tex's opinion. But not all of it. If pressed, Tex will admit that Dog-Man Tony may have done some bad things, starting when he lived in Minneapolis a few years ago.

"I told him, man, you went south on me. You went to shit. He just tells me, 'I know, Tex, I know.'"

Last July, Anthony Hugh Ross a.k.a. Dog-Man Tony was arrested in La Crosse on a warrant charging him with a Texas murder. A Texas investigator came to Wisconsin to question him. He hoped to have Dog-Man extradited on the strength of an eyewitness description of the murder. Dog-Man allegedly taunted his victim by holding a knife to his throat and saying, "I could kill you in a heartbeat," then slit his throat and said, "Oh well, another one bites the dust."

Dog-Man became a minor celebrity after being featured on "America's Most Wanted." He was released from the La Crosse jail in August after the witness in the Texas case was run over and killed by a train.

****

In August 1994, Michael Garfinkle, 20, a college student who rode the rails for kicks, was found dead with his smashed head covered along the railway tracks near Emeryville, California. Earlier that year, a vagrant named Willie Clark was found beaten to death in Tallahassee, Florida. He'd been robbed and bludgeoned with a steel pole that had concrete clumped at one end. His head was covered. Another drifter was murdered and robbed in a hobo jungle in Kansas a year later. That was shortly before the murder in Whitefish, and with a similar MO.

Those investigations were going nowhere, but the probe of an April 1995 murder in the Salt Lake City rail yards appeared more promising. Like the other victims, Roger Lee Bowman had been beaten with a blunt object, but the police had an eyewitness. The Salt Lake victim, the perpetrator, and a transient woman had been drinking and doing drugs in a hobo jungle near the tracks.

"An argument started and the lady left," detective Chuck Oliver explains. "There'd been some threats, and she had a sense that things might get violent. She told us she went to a nearby liquor store, and when she returned her boyfriend was dead. She said that a man named Brad Foster had killed him. He'd fled, of course. We believe he hopped a freight for California."

The witness described Foster as a white male in his 30s or early 40s, 6 feet tall, and weighing about 190 pounds. His dark hair was cropped short.

Meanwhile Mike Quakenbush, the Salem detective, had sent out a nationwide teletype asking other police agencies if they were aware of homicides similar to the one he was investigating. Many investigators responded, and the suspicion arose that a serial killer was at work.

Quakenbush obtained a photo of the Portland victim, Michael Clites, and showed it to transients. One recalled being with him in a homeless mission in Vancouver, Washington, on December 4, when Clites cashed a $300 disability check. Quakenbush also found a man in Vancouver who'd ridden a freight with Clites as far as Eugene, Oregon. He'd last seen Clites walking off with a man who called himself Sidetrack.

Quakenbush began spending time in the railroad yards. He hopped a few freights and talked to drifters and railroad police. Some were familiar with Sidetrack's name (some knew him as Sidetrack Bob), but none knew his whereabouts.

Sidetrack wasn't Quakenbush's only suspect. Salt Lake City investigator Oliver had given him the name and description of the suspect in their case, Brad Foster. Several other detectives told him that investigations had brought up the name Robert Silveria, not necessarily as a suspect, but as someone worth talking to.

Quakenbush sent word to railroad police all over the west coast to be on the lookout for Brad Foster, Sidetrack, and

Silveria. In early 1996, he received a call from a rail officer in Roseville, California. Silveria was in town, and police soon arrested him on a parole violation.

A few days later, Quakenbush came down to question him. He noted that Silveria was just over 6 feet and weighed about 180 pounds. Like many FTRA members, he had the word "Freedom" tattooed on his throat.

"The first thing I asked him was his train name. He said 'Sidetrack,' and that's when things clicked for me."

* * *

At the Hobo Music Festival in Marquette, Iowa, several hobos said they knew Sidetrack. They spoke of running into him in the mountain west, in Texas, and as far east as Florida. Most were only casually acquainted with him, but the Texas Madman claims to know him well. The Madman is rail-thin and hollow-cheeked. A few wisps of beard sprout from his chin, and big, sunken, blue eyes peer from his rachitic face. He wears a railroad man's cap, and a denim jacket sporting a button that says Brotherhood of Hobos of America.

"Sidetrack and I rode together for quite a little time," he says, "mostly in 1989 and '90. We rode the old Southern Pacific, looking for lumber work around Klamath Falls. He was not a bad man to ride with. He was a good cribbage player, and if we were jungled up somewhere with nothing for the Frisco, why, he'd get into a game with some of these railroad men, and pretty soon we'd have $150 or more. He was not young, but he was a strong man, over 6 foot tall. Drank vodka.

"He never struck me as the kind of person they say he is. We'd ride together for a few days, maybe up to a week or two.

One thing, though, regular as clockwork he'd disappear for a while. Wouldn't say nothing, just be gone, maybe an hour, maybe half a day. Gives me an awful feeling to think what he might have been doing, but I never felt any threat from him. Said he'd been on the rails 11 years. Had a wife and family somewhere."

"I rode out of Havre, Montana, with Sidetrack," says Tex. "Never knew what he was up to, but I'll tell you this. He drank a whole lot of vodka, and sometimes he'd black out and act kind of strange."

Choo Choo Johnson and Guitar Whitey met Sidetrack in the Portland, Oregon yards, in August 1995. The encounter is well documented. Johnson, whose real name is Donald Warner, is a retired account executive with Paine Webber who writes for Buzz Potter's Hobo Times, and takes many of the railroad pictures that grace its cover.

Sidetrack told the men his name was Paul Dykeman. He claimed to be a roofer by trade, moving from job to job via the rails. Johnson and Whitey were impressed by Dykeman's professed work ethic and his cheerful demeanor. They weren't even put off when he told them he was an FTRA member. He claimed the organization had gotten a bad name from the actions of a few. He said he'd spent five years in a penitentiary but was a reformed man.

The three of them kindled a fire, brewed some coffee, and Choo Choo asked Whitey and their new buddy to pose for a picture. They did, and the man who appears in the photo has since been positively identified by investigators as Robert Silveria a.k.a. Sidetrack. In the picture Silveria's pack is on the ground, with an ax handle protruding from it. He later told investigators that the ax handle was his weapon of choice.

* * *

With Silveria in custody, Quakenbush contacted the other police agencies investigating the murders of drifters. Detectives from Oregon, Kansas, Utah, and Florida descended on Auburn, California. Silveria spoke freely to them for days.

"It struck me that he just wanted to get a load off his mind," says Wade Harper, who was investigating the murder of the college student/hobo in nearby Emeryville. "He just calmly stated the facts, in great detail. I more or less ran out of questions. I had to ask him if I'd left anything out."

Silveria drew a map of the area where Willie Clark had been murdered two years before, for Tallahassee investigator Jeff Johnson. "You'd have thought a surveyor drew it, it was that accurate," says Johnson.

Sidetrack told Chuck Oliver, the Salt Lake investigator, that he killed in a rage. He said rage was a necessary precursor to the act, and if it didn't come upon him naturally, he would manufacture an incident that provoked a confrontation. He robbed his victims and sometimes used their ID to set up food stamp accounts.

Silveria has since recanted all his confessions and is awaiting trial in Oregon. First-degree murder charges have been filed against him in four cases; two in Oregon, one in Kansas, and one in Florida. He faces the death penalty.

"We have plenty of evidence, but we're sort of waiting in line," says Chuck Oliver of Salt Lake City, whose investigation has led him to believe his suspect, Brad Foster, is Sidetrack.

Silveria is the prime suspect in five other cases, including the Whitefish, Montana, killing, based on his confessions in jail. He spoke of eight murders in all, but investigators say they have evidence connecting him with at least 12 dating back to 1989. "He fits the serial-killer mode," says Grandinetti. "He has his little ritual. He covers their heads."

Another investigator, however, fears that Silveria is "clearing paper" for the FTRA, taking the rap for crimes other than his own. If that scenario is correct Sidetrack has made life easier for killers on the rails, but their chances of getting caught are slim anyway. Violent deaths of marginal people rank among investigators' least favorite homicides to probe. Rail riders are well aware that they are on their own. Nevertheless, empty freight cars are getting harder to find. The number of drifters who ride the rails has increased, with newcomers driven by economic forces and personal demons alike.

Tex says he can't imagine quitting, dangers notwithstanding. "I'm bipolar," he explains. "I don't take the medicine, though. It makes me sleepy. I'd rather just smoke a little reefer, or better yet, get on the train and ride. That's the best upper there is."

Postscript

In 1998, Robert Silveria—aka Sidetrack—pleaded guilty to the murders of William Pettit and Michael Clites in Oregon, a deal that allowed him to escape the death penalty. He has claimed responsibility for up to 28 murders at various times, and investigators believe he committed at least 13. As part of his agreement he gave considerable information about the FTRA. As of 2014 he was alive and doing life in prison.

The Hanged Priest

The Hanged Priest

When Father Ryan Erickson celebrated Mass at St. Patrick's Church in Hudson, Wisconsin, the show was on and he was the star. As he put it in an e-mail to his congregants, he liked his rituals "rich and mysterious," a stark change from the "orgy of handshaking and hugs" to which they'd become accustomed.

The way Erickson hoisted the host over his head and held it aloft for a minute or more made a vivid contrast to the perfunctory elevation that the senior priests favored. Tears rolled down his cheeks during the ceremony. The monk's cassock he affected billowed theatrically, hiding the bulge at his waist from the pistol he packed there.

Erickson's energetic performance got mixed reviews from his audience. The parishioners who were wowed by his histrionics became known as "kneelers," because they knelt during Consecration. The "standers" were either uncomfortable with his act or oblivious. Mostly they suffered in silence. Many opted to attend another church. Their parish's spiritual life, they believed, was being hijacked by the born-agains, people they wearily referred to as "holy rollers" in reference to their fervor. They also called them "chirpers," after a retreat group that Father Ryan led named Christ Renews His Parish, or CRHP.

Among the standers was 39-year-old Dan O'Connell, a member of one of Hudson's most prominent families, and owner of the O'Connell Funeral Home. O'Connell was married and had two elementary school-aged children. Several generations of his family had worshiped at St. Patrick's, and Dan did too, but he wasn't particularly religious. Gregarious and sociable, secular activities were more his thing. He was a Rotarian and a volunteer ambulance attendant. He served hot dogs at the annual North Hudson Pepper Fest and rode in the Dutch Days parade in nearby Baldwin. Not much went on in Hudson that he didn't hear about. He saw the schism in his church firsthand every Sunday. He may have fretted about it privately, but people on both sides were buried out of his funeral home and he had no interest in getting involved.

On February 5, 2002, O'Connell and his 22-year-old intern, James Ellison, were shot to death in O'Connell's office. The crime shocked the community because murders are so unusual in Hudson, and because one of the victims was such a prominent person.

The police had no real suspects three days later, when O'Connell's funeral was held at St. Patrick's. Among the priests taking part in the ceremony was Father Ryan, dressed in simple white vestments and behaving with uncharacteristic restraint. He said a quiet homily.

Unbeknownst to the mourners and the police, Father Ryan had exchanged tense words with Dan O'Connell the day before the killings, an incident that left the priest shaken. Investigators wouldn't find out about it for more than two years.

A county medical examiner had discovered the bodies and called the police in the early afternoon, while he was visiting the funeral home to pick up a death certificate. The scene of the crime clearly suggested that O'Connell had been the target. He was shot to death where he was sitting, behind his desk. Ellison had risen from his chair and was bolting for the door when he was shot in the back. Investigators theorized that an argument between O'Connell and the perpetrator had erupted into sudden violence. Ellison was apparently murdered because he was a witness.

Intern James Ellison seemed to be the forgotten victim in a crime that was invariably described in news reports as, "the O'Connell slaying." According to his family he was a hard-working, good-natured young man. They were touched by a scrapbook of reminiscences put together by his classmates at the University of Minnesota indicating how well-liked he'd been.

Initially, the police looked into a Wisconsin-based cult, Rest of Jesus, which objects to embalming, but quickly decided they were harmless eccentrics. Investigators also pursued the possibility that crazed potheads might have been ransacking the mortuary for embalming fluid to spike their marijuana, but the idea didn't stand up to scrutiny. "You don't need a license to buy embalming fluid," said Hudson Police Chief Richard Trende, "and it's not expensive. There was just no evidence to support that theory."

In fact there was no evidence to support any theory, but there were plenty of rumors. One of them had O'Connell and his intern returning to the mortuary and discovering the perpetrator in flagrante delicto with a corpse. Another involved Father Ryan, but only peripherally. Shortly after the 9/11 attacks O'Connell had helped organize a fundraiser for the victims, a spaghetti dinner at St. Patrick's. There was suspicion that he'd discovered someone stealing cash. Father Ryan had helped out with the dinner, but again, there was no evidence that any money was missing. There was only gossip.

If the investigators had been looking carefully, they might have noticed that the church itself seemed to be a center of intrigue. There were threats against the church school's principal, who'd resigned under the sustained assault of Father Ryan's most fervent followers. There was Father Ryan's gun collection and his history of binge drinking. Something had happened to this once-peaceful 150-year-old parish to cleave it down the middle, and Father Ryan was the central figure in the conflict.

For two years, the questions continued, until October 2005, when St. Croix County Attorney Eric Johnson presented evidence connecting Father Ryan to the murders. Johnson offered an explanation for what Erickson and O'Connell were talking about in the minutes before the murder. In doing so he confirmed what had long been suspected by Erickson's critics, that the crusading sexual moralist had been engaging in the kind of crimes that have devastated the Catholic Church in recent years.

Father Ryan didn't answer those charges. In December 2004 he hung himself in an open skyway connecting the two buildings of St. Mary's of the Seven Dolors, in Hurley, Wisconsin, the church where he'd been reassigned as a senior priest. Startled townspeople saw his body swinging in the icy wind that morning. It stayed there on display for several hours while the local authorities dithered, and conferred with the archdiocese about how to deal with the situation.

His suicide came the day after investigators executed a search warrant on his living quarters, looking for evidence that would connect him to the murders. Among other things, they discovered child pornography on his computer, some of it involving bondage.

****

Ryan Erickson grew up in Campbellsport, Wisconsin. After his parents moved when he was in his early teens, he went to live with a priest, and spent summers with his family at a campground in Eagle River, Wisconsin. How he comported himself there became the subject of some of the rumors about Erickson's sexual preferences that swirled around Hudson after his suicide. But "The Hanged Priest," as he'd come to be known, still had defenders.

Tim Schemel, who resides in Florida, wrote (In Renew America, a right wing web magazine) that he doesn't believe that "Ryan could have or would have the means to murder anyone." Schemel, who spent summers at the same campground as Erickson, claimed he heard rumors of alleged sexual improprieties involving Erickson back then, but Erickson never made any advances toward him. "He never touched me, due to the fact that I would have killed him, friend or no friend," wrote Schemel.

Another summer resident at the campground got a different picture of young Ryan. "He was 18 when we knew him," says a fiftyish woman from Wausakee, Wisconsin. "My son was 14, and all the kids ran around together. It was pretty obvious to me that Ryan was gay. He talked constantly about becoming a priest, and I just assumed it was because he didn't want to come out to his parents. They hung around the bar most of the time, and his father seemed kind of ill-tempered.

"How did I know he was gay? His attitude toward girls, for one thing. He was a good-looking kid, and the girls were always flirting with him, but he wouldn't have anything to do with them, which I can tell you is quite unusual for an 18-year-old boy. He said it was because of his calling. He said that someday he'd be 'Father Ryan.'"

Like several sources contacted for this story, the woman insisted on anonymity because she feared Erickson's followers.

"You couldn't help liking him," she said. "He was very charming, and kind of mischievous. I didn't care if he was gay. My son would've known how to handle it if he ever hit on him, but that never happened. My son did warn me not to let our eight-year-old grandson go off alone with Ryan. He didn't say why. He didn't have to."

The only thing that really bothered her about young Ryan was his heavy drinking. She says that he got a job stocking the campground's bar, but was caught stealing booze and fired. After that incident he was never seen at the campground again.

Erickson's classmates at St. Paul's Seminary in Minneapolis referred to him as "the Monsignor" because of his ultra-conservative religious views. After being ordained in June 2000, he was assigned to St. Patrick's in Hudson. Pictures of him taken around that time show a baby-faced, bespectacled young man with a dour expression.

He came to St. Patrick's with some firm beliefs: that levity had no place in sermons; that Mass should be celebrated at least partly in Latin; and that it was his calling to lecture parishioners, especially children, about mortal sin. In a simpler age, more experienced priests might have channeled Father Ryan's energy into something productive, and lightened up his dark side. Instead, aging head priest Peter Szleszinski left him to find his own niche, and Father Ryan became the instigator of a parish-wide struggle that fed his messianic impulses. He quickly took a leadership role in the CRHP group. Many of the born-agains who attended his retreats had children in St. Patrick's school, and it was there that Father Ryan gravitated.

Principal Pat Brandner welcomed him at first. Brandner was a few years from retirement in the Medford, Wisconsin, public schools when she decided to take the job at St. Patrick's. She'd been an academic counselor at Medford, but she had an MA in theology and wanted to join the parochial school system.

From the beginning, Brandner needed all the help she could get. She'd arrived the same year as Erickson, and had quickly run afoul of a group of parents who took exception to some curriculum changes, especially a reorganization of math classes. The argument broke down to the parents' "conservative" approach versus the principal's "liberal" pedagogical style. Before this conflict was played out, Brandner would be harassed, intimidated, and physically attacked.

One of Father Ryan's chores at St. Patrick's School was sex education. His supporters liked the priest's black-and-white approach to the topic, but other parents were alarmed by what he told their kids. Mortal sins and the temptation to commit them were his major concern. Abortion was high on his list, but it was trumped by masturbation, which obsessed him. He later expressed himself on the topic in a "thought for the day" e-mailed to his followers:

"Even Sunday Mass is not safe from the immodest dress of some devils. They come to read, give out Holy Communion, etc. looking like an advertisement. There [sic] immodest dress says to all present: I'm easy! Please go home and masturbate to my beautiful body. The sad thing is that some do."

Father Ryan's reference to church-going Catholic women as "devils" must have struck some on his e-mail list as odd, but nobody doubted that he got his details about rampant onanism firsthand. Father Ryan aggressively sought adolescent and pre-adolescent confessional visitors. He instructed the students at St. Patrick's school to come to him for confession, and got pushy if they were reluctant. Why haven't you seen Father this week? he asked several junior high students.

The conservatives wanted Father Ryan to take a larger role at the school, but Brandner soon began to doubt whether he should be there at all. (Brandner did not return calls for this story.) She was supported by parents who didn't want him to come near their children.

"Pat overheard him in communion class, and what he was teaching really concerned her," says a parishioner with knowledge of the situation. "It was all this negative, pre-Vatican II stuff."

The division in St. Patrick's Church developed at the same time as the problems in the school. Patricia German, who identifies herself as a follower of Father Ryan, argues that the split came from some congregants' resistance to the hard truths that he taught.

"I know that Father's frank discussion of mortal sin offended some people, but he simply preached the real teachings of the church," German says. "They'd been hearing a watered-down version of the faith until he came. He taught the true faith and it made some uncomfortable. I'd say the parish was about 10 percent with us, 10 percent opposed, and the rest pretty uninvolved."

A woman who was on the other side of the rift questions whether it's that simple. She uses the example of the kneeling/standing controversy. "Bishops have a wide latitude concerning what they can do in the diocese, and Father Peter, with the Bishop's tacit approval, allowed people to stand during Consecration, because the ones in back couldn't see if they knelt. It was a minor thing, a matter of convenience, but it became this huge, divisive argument, the kneelers versus the standers."

Father Ryan's critics said he wanted to drag their church back to the 12th century, but he was quite modern in one respect—he used his extensive e-mail list to exhort the faithful, and chastise the infidels. At his urging the faithful demanded militant action against abortion and gay sex, calling public opposition to such sins a religious duty. During the run-up to the 2004 election they distributed leaflets in the church parking lot demanding that Catholics vote for George Bush, another duty of the faith.

Patricia German's husband, Jerry, says that Father Ryan brought passion to St. Patrick's, something that had been sorely lacking until then. "He did everything passionately," German says. "Preach, hunt, fish, drink beer. He just reeked passion."

Father Ryan and a group of men he hung out with, most of them St. Patrick's parishioners, got together and drank beer at bars in Hudson once a week. The topics of conversation were "the usual" according to one of them: "Guns, gays, hunting, how everything's going to hell."

By September 2001, Brandner was losing her hold on the school. The parents who opposed her had leafleted cars in the church parking lot demanding her resignation, and had taken their concerns to the diocese. She had many supporters, but they had neither the zeal nor the activist presence of her detractors, and the constant agitation against her was beginning to take a toll on her health.

A confrontation with a parent named Helen Shaw put her over the edge. It was characterized as a physical attack in the Hudson newspaper.

"I did not assault her," says Shaw. "I'd been asked to drive some kids to a retreat by one of the teachers. I was in the hall when I saw her, and to this day I don't know why she called 911. I think it was a well-thought-out deal. She was bucking to get rid of several parents, including me. And she wanted to get rid of Father Ryan too. I didn't like that, but I did not assault her."

Queried about the animosity between herself and Brandner, Shaw claims it was probably due to her own inquisitiveness.

"At the time all this happened I'd just come to my faith, and I had question upon question upon question," she explains. "I'd been Catholic my entire life but I actually hadn't found my faith until I went on a retreat called Christ Renews His Parish, and I realized there were many things I didn't know. I was questioning her and some of the teachers about why religion wasn't being thoroughly taught in school. Pat Brandner had a 'how dare you question me' attitude.

"Father Ryan affected me very deeply," says Shaw. "What he did was make me aware of my faith, which is a very deep faith that requires lots of study and research to understand. He enlightened me. You'd invite him over for dinner and he'd just talk. He wouldn't even eat. He just loved the faith. He explained mortal sin to me, and I really didn't understand that before. It's different than a venial sin, which is something that can be forgiven at Mass."

Shaw explains that mortal sins can be forgiven if they're confessed, but there is a price to pay for committing them knowingly. "Father brought them to light," she says. "He explained what mortal sins are, and if you turn around and do them again when you know it's a sin, then your soul is in trouble."

Shaw knows that Erickson came to be viewed as a divisive figure, but she didn't see him that way. "People turned it into something divisive. He taught the truth, and there are a lot of people who don't want to hear it. He stuck to his guns. The truth is the truth and there is no variance. For example, looking at pornographic material is a sin. Well, there are a lot of men in our parish who look at girlie magazines, and they don't want to hear that. Abortion is a sin. Masturbation is a sin. They don't want to hear that, because they've gone through it, or maybe they're for it."

A parishioner who resented Erickson's single-minded vision took exception to that explanation of what split the parish. "Telling adults that certain behavior is sinful is part of a priest's job description," she says, "but it was all hell and damnation with him. Never a word about joy or forgiveness. Sin was all he wanted to talk about. Most people get tired of that, no matter what they believe."

According to Shaw, not only gay sex, but simply being gay, is a sin. "It's a choice," she says. "That's been proven. I've read studies on it." She explains that people who aren't attracted to the opposite sex may be meant to be celibate. She finds rumors that Erickson was gay laughable. "He was a very holy priest," she says.

Asked how she could be so sure about the priest's sexual orientation, Shaw replies, "I'm a mom, and you just know these things. My kids were very close with Father Ryan. They went to his night prayers, they fished with him, they hung out with him. He was at our house all the time. When a priest comes into your life like that and he's young, you think, 'Oh-oh, better be careful.' You watch for signs, you pop into rooms, and never even once did I come close to thinking there was even a possibility."

Shaw says she was glad and relieved when Brandner resigned early in 2002. It was during the turmoil leading up to her resignation that O'Connell and Ellison were murdered. Police would later ask Erickson to account for his whereabouts when the shootings occurred. He said that he was at St. Patrick's school, and a sign-in sheet placed him there. But no one could recall seeing him.

Erickson had always been weepy during services. His supporters took it as a sign of passion, but his detractors thought he had a screw loose. After the murders his behavior became much more erratic. In September 2003, just before he was assigned to another parish, startled parishioners who entered the St. Patrick's sacristy found him howling and weeping about the sins of abortion and masturbation. At least a few of them complained to the diocese about this episode, and some believe that his reassignment, initially as an assistant priest in Ladysmith, Wisconsin, came as a direct result. Others say it was simply routine.

* * *

In August 2005, Hudson investigator Jeff Knopp and police chief Richard Trende announced that evidence they'd collected tying Erickson to the murders would be presented at a closed hearing. At a press conference, County Attorney Eric Johnson said that he would review the evidence, go over it with the victims' families, and then make it public. As the weeks passed, rumors about Father Ryan, including some that had begun around the time of the murders, continued to circulate.

One that persisted didn't involve the killings. It concerned a medieval twist on church politics. St. Patrick's head priest Peter Szleszinski was stricken with a mysterious illness a few months before Father Ryan was reassigned. He didn't respond to treatment, and his life seemed to be in danger, but shortly after Father Ryan left for Ladysmith he recovered just as mysteriously as he'd fallen ill. Szleszinski retired in apparent good health in January 2005. Some of Father Ryan's critics wondered if he was trying to poison his way to the top. He'd made no secret of his desire to take over at St. Patrick's, and even did so unofficially when Father Peter left on a vacation during Father Ryan's tenure.

"He just stepped in and acted like he was the head priest," says a parishioner. "He found himself a monsignor's outfit and started wearing it. It really looked ludicrous on a baby-faced young man. It was like a Saturday Night Live routine."

Despite the intrigue and the rumors, investigators didn't get interested in Father Ryan as a suspect until November 2004, when he was being questioned about alleged child abuse and volunteered his theory of the murders. According to evidence made public in 2005, he implicated himself by revealing knowledge about the crime scene that only the perpetrator and investigators would know. They confronted him about his knowledge; he claimed a detective had told him the details. When that investigator denied it, Father Ryan suggested it may have been another cop, who denied it as well.

There was a lot more connecting Father Ryan to the murders than familiarity with the scene. He drove a car resembling the one witnesses saw leaving the funeral home at the time of the murders, and he fit a description of the driver. Investigators went over his computer, and also held e-mails and links to websites related to pedophilia as evidence.

A confrontation between Father Ryan and O'Connell the day before the murder in which O'Connell threatened to reveal the Priest as a child abuser is described in the evidence. After Father Ryan hung himself, a Hurley, Wisconsin, deacon told investigators that Erickson had confessed to the crime, saying, "I've done it."

Father Ryan's suicide complicated the investigation into his child abuse. According to one source familiar with the investigation, some of the child victims came from conservative Catholic families who were reluctant to believe Father Ryan had abused their kids. They impeded the investigation, and until it was complete, investigators couldn't fill in the blanks concerning Father Ryan's motive for murdering O'Connell. According to the same source, some of the victims "came of age" and began talking to investigators on their own. One 20-year-old witness testified that Erickson gave him alcohol and fondled him at the St. Patrick's rectory.

The closing of the case came as a great relief to most of Hudson's citizens, but Father Ryan's hard-core supporters found it difficult to accept. When pressed, these people would admit that "the hanged priest" hung himself, but they also hinted at a mysterious martyrdom. In death as in life he remains a divisive figure—either murdered or hounded to an early grave by demonic liberals according to his devotees; dead of a self-imposed penance after a subconsciously compelled confession according to his critics.

One of his followers, Darla Meyers, has become a regular on right-wing talk shows and the far-right web media, where she frequently invokes the memory of Father Ryan during her discussions of abortion. Meyers is the gatekeeper of a secretive website devoted to Erickson's memory. Anyone can get to the home page at fatherryanerickson.com, but only the chosen make it into the messages section, where Erickson's disciples share their memories of the man who had such an impact on their lives. Requests for a password to the inner sanctum are answered with a query: How did you know Father? Journalists are not welcome.

Occasionally, though, tributes to Erickson make their way onto Matt Abbott's Renew America website, and into the public domain:

"The man was incredible. The first mass he said that I attended he cried when he consecrated the host. I thought I was going to also. The reverence that man had for the Eucharist was breathtaking."

"What a picture, a 31-year-old man wearing a cassock. His vestments were beautiful. He dabbled in Latin in the Mass, but the convent of liberal nuns were none-too-happy with that. Didn't stop him though."

"Unless a suicide note was left behind in the priest's handwriting, I would be cautious about labeling this a suicide. With a murder investigation involving the priest underway, I think it not beyond the realm of possibility that someone murdered the priest by hanging him in order for it to appear to be a suicide. I hope this case is thoroughly investigated. Sometimes the obvious answer is not the correct one."

"Wait until all the facts are in. Setting up a fall guy to stop a murder investigation is not so far-fetched."

Helen Shaw's attitude mirrors that of many of Erickson's supporters. She is aware that Father Ryan suffered from depression and she believes he was pushed into committing suicide. "I know that they questioned him about sexual acts with kids and I think when they did that his heart about fell through the floor. This man loved kids."

She does not believe Father Ryan committed any of the transgressions attributed to him. Amid all the newspaper coverage and the lurid details, has she ever questioned the holiness of "the hanged priest?"

"No," she says, "never."

A NOTE ON MY SOURCES

A Note On My Sources

One spring morning in 1965 I walked across the bridge from Nuevo Laredo, Mexico to Laredo, Texas with a small quantity of marijuana. It was all that remained of a larger quantity, call it a pound, that my friends Pete, Sully, Marv and I bought from an "hombre de playa" in Acapulco three months earlier. We didn't want that much but there was no point haggling. It only cost twenty dollars.

The four of us smoked plenty, and shared the rest with anyone who was looking for a good time. We even shared some with a "bandido" we encountered on an isolated stretch of beach near the then-tiny town of Zihuatanejo, a tall, skinny guy with a bandana tied around his head like a do-rag. He'd posted himself on a narrow strip of sand between the ocean and a pile of rocks, with a walking stick in one hand and a fish-ing knife in the other. "Cincuenta para pasar," he demanded, but we came around the rocks into his view one at a time, and by the time he saw there were four of us it was more a panhandle than a mugging. He told us about the hard life of a bandit, and showed us some fish he'd caught using his walking stick, a bent pin and some string for a fishing line. We offered him a handful of weed, which he wrapped in his bandana, and, we later heard, sold for 12 pesos a joint to a band of German tourists who were living in tents a few miles down the coast, on a deserted stretch of beach called Ixtapa.

We had cheap rooms in Zihuatanejo. The Hotel Irma needed paying guests badly. Earlier that winter they'd rented the whole place out to a couple of Harvard faculty members and their hippie friends, who were starting something called the International Federation for Internal Freedom (IFIF). It was FIF when they were headquartered in Cambridge, but they found out that psilocybin mushrooms could be purchased at the market in Zihuatanejo and went international. The quest for internal freedom was going well until the Federal Police got wind of what was happening, and threw them all out of Mexico because the organizers, Timothy Leary and Richard Alpert, didn't have a work permit.

The Irma emptied overnight. We arrived a few days later. Our rooms were small, sparse and smelled of Pachouli oil. Occasionally someone would wander in looking for IFIF, hang out with us and smoke some of our weed for a few days.

Despite our generosity and our wastrel ways the stash was barely half-depleted by spring. The balance fell to me because the others left for home before I did. I remember standing in the yard of the Flecha Roja bus line in Nuevo Laredo, wondering whether I should throw it away. I suppose I decided to take it across because I didn't want the fiesta to end.

As soon as the Customs officer said "step over here" I knew the jig was up.

The Webb County jail, where I arrived a short time later, was "a trip," as we said back then. There were about 200 men jammed into twenty cramped cells that were arranged around a day room with long tables and benches where we ate, speakers for a radio that played constantly, a little black and white TV and a toilet. There were urinals in the cells, but that toilet was the only one in the block, and it was located smack dab in the middle of the day room without so much as a curtain to draw around it.

Lots of Mexican illegals were being held in Webb County, so I worked on my Spanish. It wasn't long before I could tell my sad tale without stumbling, and understand several variations of the question it always prompted: Why didn't you just walk across the river? It's about two feet deep there, they explained.

All day long a radio station that called itself "the voice of the Rio Grande" played over the speakers. The big hit was She's About A Mover, by The Sir Douglas Quintet, a Texas group that was getting national attention. This was the era of the British Invasion, and if you wanted to be a rock star it helped to Anglicize. Sir Douglas was Doug Sahm from San Antonio. Some of my fellow prisoners knew him. He later recorded a few gems: *Me and Paul* ("well they said we looked suspicious, but I think they like t'pick on me and Paul"), a really soulful version of *Laredo Rose* (solo, not the one with The Texas Tornados), but I grew weary of *She's About a Mover*. It played over and over again.

One day Sir Doug sent out "a big hello to the boys in Webb County." That raised our morale awhile.

We spent all day in the day room, and nights in cells that slept four men but housed up to ten, depending on fluctuations in population. Bunks were acquired on the basis of seniority. I made bail before I got one. The floor space under the reeking urinal attached to the back wall was where you started. By the end, 32 days later, I was up near the door, where some air stirred occasionally.

Marijuana busts were an industry in Laredo, and the legal system was a racket. A guard slipped me a list of lawyers shortly after I was booked. When I was formally charged a few days later, the magistrate solemnly advised me to look over that list carefully, and spend every nickel I had on a good lawyer.

The shyster I ended up with gave me the standard advice: Plead guilty to a legal fiction, violation of The Marihuana Tax Act of 1937. If I did, he was pretty sure he could get the other two charges—smuggling and possession—dropped. Those charges carried mandatory five year minimum sentences without the possibility of parole, but there was no minimum sentence or parole restriction attached to the Tax Act. You might get probation, he said, and even if you don't you'll be eligible for parole after serving one/third of your sentence.

The tax charge rested on the assumption that upon crossing the border a rational person would present himself to a Customs officer, state that he was in possession of marijuana and ask to pay the tax. You'd be ratting on yourself, that was obvious, but I knew nothing about constitutional law and the only advice my lawyer offered was make the deal. I paused long enough to do the math and agreed, even though it sounded fishy, especially since they had me dead to rights on smuggling and possession.

As I would learn, the industry depended on that plea. There were dozens, sometimes more than 100 busts for marijuana per week at the Laredo crossing, and they all had to be processed smoothly through the legal system. Parole-eligible sentences were the carrot. Long sentences were the stick.

Parole was abolished in the federal prison system in 1987. That would have killed the Laredo marijuana racket in any case, but it was squashed long before that. A few months after I was busted, Timothy Leary and his 18-year-old daughter were turned away when they tried to enter Mexico at Laredo (that work permit violation again). When they re-entered the U.S., a joint was discovered in Leary's daughter's pocket. Leary took responsibility, but refused to cop a plea. A jury found him guilty, and District Judge Ben C. Connally gave him 30 years. He called Leary "a menace to the country" at sentencing.

Leary appealed, claiming that the Marihuana Tax Act was in violation of the Fifth Amendment, which states that "no person shall be compelled in any criminal case to be a witness against himself." The Supreme Court agreed, and vacated his sentence in 1969. He was re-tried for smuggling, convicted, and Connally gave him ten years without parole. He was serving that sentence when The Weather Underground broke him out of prison and spirited him off to Algeria.

As for me, I returned to Laredo in September 1965, to go through the charade that made the industry so profitable. No federal judge was stationed in town, but one held court there quarterly to clean up the docket. Two appearances were required before a plea could be entered. Thus, along with additional legal fees, you were required to spend anywhere from 10 days to three weeks in Laredo, renting a room, eating at restaurants, doing what you could to amuse yourself (my lawyer's advice was stay on the U.S. side in order to demonstrate that I understood the gravity of my situation). The whole town was in on the scam.

Time passed like a kidney stone in Laredo. You'd spend all day in the courtroom, one billable hour after another, hoping your name would be called. My lawyer claimed he was working tirelessly to get the prosecutor to drop the smuggling and possession charges, and to convince the judge, Ben C. Connally as it happened, to show leniency for the tax conviction.

Of course, dropping the smuggling and possession charges was a foregone conclusion. The industry was based on it. As for the latter, leniency is a relative term, and in my case it was relative to the kind of sentence Leary received.

I tried not to dwell on the possibility of prison, but there wasn't much to do in the courtroom except watch the clock and that always got the wheels turning. You couldn't even hear what was going on unless you were seated up front. Every 15 minutes or so the bailiff would shout out a docket number. A shyster would materialize out of some sanctum where they hid, and motion to his client, who would make his way to the bench.

The two of them would stand before the judge. An inaudible conversation would ensue. Maybe some documents would change hands. After a while the judge would pound his gavel. Lawyer and client would go their separate ways, and the bailiff would shout another name. Occasionally there was a little drama when someone was taken away in chains. Otherwise it was hours of stupefying boredom.

Only once was the tedium interrupted by anything out of the ordinary. A Texas Ranger burst into the courtroom one afternoon, had a quick conference with the judge, and they exited into chambers.

"Clear the courtroom," shouted the bailiff.

Normally, two factions formed in the hall during a recess: racketeers at one end, mingling and networking like they were at a trade show; marijuana sinners at the other end, talking amongst ourselves. But this time more Texas Rangers were waiting outside the courtroom, and they shooed all of us, prosecutors, defendants, lawyers, outside like so many flies. "Hurry, hurry," they said.

We emerged into the blazing sun, and stood there blinking, bewildered by what we saw. Both sides of that usually quiet street were lined with soldiers, rifles at the ready. The clatter of a chopper hovering at rooftop level battered our ears. Gritty air stirred up by the rotors stung our eyes. Stay back! a soldier warned. You couldn't hear him, but he made his point by jabbing in our direction with his bayonet.

A caravan of armored vehicles swept past led by a squad car with rotating emergency lights, and disappeared into a garage. A few minutes later, the Rangers gave word that we could return to the courtroom. By then the chopper was gone, and the soldiers were at ease. I asked a Ranger what was going on, but he wouldn't answer.

Next day during a recess a black guy about my age introduced himself. His name was Connor. You here for the tax count? he said. So'm I.

Prison ain't so bad, he added.

Say what? It sounded pretty bad to me. I told him my lawyer said I might get probation. He shook his head and smiled. Ain't nobody gettin' probation, he said.

He seemed to know what he was talking about, which didn't exactly cheer me up. He proceeded to explain something else my counsel hadn't bothered to mention. There were two kinds of sentences: the B Sentence, which meant you were eligible for parole after serving one/third of your time; and the A Sentence, which meant you were eligible immediately. Connor was hoping for an A sentence, maybe two or three years, which might result in six to eight months served, then parole.

Eight months in prison, I thought. If that's as bad it gets I can do it.

Connor had another revelation. Them soldiers an' all yesterday? That was for Frenchy. Government'a Canada fell count'a him.

He said "Frenchy" was being held at a nearby military base because there was a price on his head. How does he know these things? I wondered. I was skeptical, but the next day an article appeared in the Laredo paper about the "unprecedented" military presence that accompanied a man, said to be Canadian, who was in federal court testifying. It didn't mention any governments falling.

I wasn't aware at the time, but that was a good lesson about scuttlebutt. Courtroom gossip and jailhouse rumors usually embellish the truth a bit, but they are essentially true nonetheless. The only exception is the occasional piece of disinformation planted by the authorities.

After 17 days in Laredo I made my last appearance in court, and didn't waste any time leaving town. A registered letter arrived one month later, summoning me to Houston for sentencing. Judge Ben C. Connally gave me five years, and denied my request for an A sentence.

My heart sank, but after a few hours in the Harris County Jail, a genuine hell-hole, my lawyer performed the only real service he ever provided. He got a request in front of the judge for 30 days to settle my affairs. It was granted and I was released. I felt like I'd died and gone to heaven.

It was evening by the time I got to the Houston airport. There were no direct flights to Minneapolis until morning, and I wanted out of Texas badly, so I caught a plane to Chicago.

We were circling to land at O'Hare, when suddenly the engines revved and we swooped back upward. Everyone was pinned to their seats. After we leveled out, the intercom crackled, and the pilot explained that a warning light had come on indicating "a little problem with the landing gear." He said it would be straightened out quickly.

A woman began sobbing a few rows away. The man next to me had our mutual armrest in a death grip. I silently rooted for a crash, from which I saw myself emerging miraculously whole, swapping wallets with the smoldering remains of one of my fellow passengers and running for dear life.

No such luck. We landed safely a few minutes later.

At 8 a.m. on the day after Thanksgiving, 1965, I surrendered to the U.S. Marshals. I was immediately chained to another unfortunate soul who'd turned himself in at the same time, a plain Midwestern-looking guy wearing a white shirt and gray dress slacks. His name was Ron.

Ron was the same age as me, 26, but the resemblance ended there. This was the dawning of the age of hair, and mine was brown and longish in the early Beatles style. Ron's was sandy and buzz-cut like a Marine's. He looked at me apologetically as the shackles snapped shut. I nodded to let him know it wasn't his fault. They gave us about a foot of slack so we wouldn't trip over each other, frog-marched us down to the garage, placed us in the back seat of a van and transported us to the Federal Correctional Institution at Sandstone, 100 miles north of the Twin Cities.

The trip took two hours. On the way up, Ron told me that he'd embezzled some money from a local credit union, where he was an up-and-coming loan officer—"twenty thousand dollars, give or take." He was doing a year and a day on the A plan, figured to do about six months.

I didn't share the details of how I'd come to grief. I did tell him my sentence. He shook his head sympathetically. I guess I'm lucky, he said. But I am truly and sincerely ashamed of what I did.

I was about to tell him I wasn't, but decided against it. It seemed to me the hum of the tires created a false sense of privacy. I saw the Marshal looking at us in the rear view mirror a few times, and he must have overheard. I think Ron was counting on that.

I was dumbstruck anyway, having had a bit to drink the night before and being in a state of existential shock.

Ron explained that the extra day beyond a year he'd received meant he'd been sentenced as a felon, so it might be tough getting a job in his chosen field when he got out. Too bad, I commiserated. He wondered if I'd have the same problem. I haven't chosen one yet, I said.

Ron probably thought I was tardy in that respect, while in my opinion he'd failed to take advantage of the prolonged adolescence all Americans had coming back then. It hardly mattered. Both our careers would be languishing awhile.

We exited the freeway, drove down a winding county road through some woods, passed through an electronic gate, and there was Sandstone Prison—an old, Victorian-looking former insane asylum that functioned as the administration center, and five wooden barracks around a yard, surrounded by chain link fence. There were gun towers at the four corners of the fence.

The Marshal escorted us into I&D - Intake and Discharge (what a chasm that ampersand stood for).

The intake process began with me signing something I didn't bother reading, then being taken into a small room for a strip-search and a squirt in the privates from a flit gun clearly labeled DDT. That was a first for me. The guard saw the look on my face. It's on the paper you signed, he said. Permission? We don't want lice and crabs and such here.

They shaved our heads, took our pictures and had us sign receipts for our clothes and the few small items we'd foolishly taken with us. Nothing from outside was allowed inside. Wallets, cash, keys, pencils, etc. all would be sent to "next of kin," a term that struck me as unnecessarily funereal. My girlfriend ended up with mine, and I lost them forever because she wasn't my girlfriend any more when I got out, but that's another story.

The clothes we wore would be laundered, sorted for size and given to other inmates when they were discharged we were told. And there would be clothes for us when we made it to the other side of the ampersand. Meanwhile, they gave us prison blues, and a pair of ugly brown shoes (that same girlfriend visited me a few weeks later and called them "Elmer Fudd shoes," which, I'm proud to say, became standard lingo during my stay at Sandstone). A guard escorted us down an echoing corridor to A&O—Adjustment & Orientation—the cell house where we would stay for a month before being placed in the general population.

Ron and I shared a cell. They told us to stay there while our paperwork was finished, then we were free to walk around the cell house hall or sit in the day room. Thus did I become acquainted with the fundamental dilemma, doing time. That first afternoon stretched out like the Sahara. There was no way to cross it but you had to get across.

I watched TV for a while. I chatted with Ron. I chatted with Frank, a teamster from Ohio who was Jimmy Hoffa's rap partner, and asked him what kind of guy Hoffa was. He laughed. I don't know, I never met him, he said.

Frank's crime consisted of signing off on a loan that a lieutenant of Hoffa's had approved. He introduced another Teamster, a black guy from Detroit named Lester.

Yeah, I know Jimmy, he said. Jimmy's hard as nails. Good man, but Bobby Kennedy sure don't like him.

A skinny little guy was sitting at a table by himself, rolling up cigarettes from a package of Indian tobacco. That's administrative segregation up there, he said, nodding toward a stairway with a gate across the landing. You know, the hole. They got'em a snitch up there right now, for his own protection. Hell, we'd kill a man like him some'a the places I been.

He told us his name was Vern. He looked like a wino—sunken cheeks, greasy hair, nose webbed with broken blood vessels. He smiled a knowing little smile that revealed three or four teeth that still clung to his gums.

Vern had some interesting information, but there was something off-putting about his tone. In retrospect, he was my introduction to the institutionalized personality. His CV was classic, a series of short stretches for minor crimes, starting when he was a juvenile. Life on the installment plan.

High profile informants were routinely housed at Sandstone, Vern explained, due to its remote location, plus another quirk of sentencing of which we had yet to be officially informed, "mandatory good time." Ten days per month were shaved off your sentence if you weren't "written up" for any serious infractions. Since nobody who was doing more than five years was assigned to a "correctional institution" like Sandstone, good time could take a significant chunk off your sentence. Therefore, the inmates tended to behave themselves.

According to Vern, men who were doing decades if not life at penitentiaries like Atlanta and Leavenworth had their own code, and they didn't care about good time. Snitch's life ain't worth a pack'a store boughts in them places, he said, a clear reference to the upstairs tenant.

That night, night one, something woke me up. You couldn't see your hand in front of your face inside the cell, but a moonlit gun tower was visible through the barred window.

Ron was awake too. You hear that? he asked.

I didn't know if I had or not, but moments later it came again, the sound of metal banging and grating against metal, and a muffled voice - *Hey! Goddam you let me out!* More slamming and grating. *Hear me fock-air! I want out from here!*

A guard shined his light through the hatch and saw that we were awake. That's Frenchy up there, he said. I guess he's trying to tear the radiator out of the wall. Hell, that's not humanly possible. He'll quiet down soon.

He did quiet down, but not soon. Did that name, "Frenchy," register? I don't think so.

Just as I was drifting off again the noise resumed. This time it ended with a THUNK that made the walls shiver. Then footsteps and shouts in the corridor.

Now the moon was shining directly through the window. Soon I could see water flowing in under the cell door. As I watched, one of my Elmer Fudds came unmoored and floated toward the back wall.

Mop pails rolled up and down the hall all night. The floor was still wet next morning. Later that day the Warden relented, and Frenchy came downstairs to mix with the A&O prisoners.

He was a little bull of a man, about 5'5", with fair skin, craggy features and a big, square jaw. The crazed gleam in his eyes dimmed a bit after he'd been out of the hole a few days, but he still looked like he could kill you with a head butt. There were burns on his hands from the radiator.

At first we didn't know how to treat him, but human nature gradually took over. I broke the ice by asking him about the Laredo incident. Sure, sure, that was me, he said. More guys gathered around as he told his story.

According to him, he was no run-of-the-mill snitch. He was the one who'd been betrayed, and by God he was getting even.

He told us he was a burglar from Montreal. A fence there had introduced him to Lucien Rivard, the head of organized crime in Canada. Rivard had hired him to pick up a car in Mexico City, and drive it to Bridgeport, Connecticut. He was instructed to cross at Laredo between four and six p.m. on a certain day, when the Customs officers would be bribed. He did as he was instructed, but was busted nevertheless, with just shy of 100 pounds of heroin stuffed in the backrest of the driver's seat. The estimated value of his cargo was $50 million. He was looking at 30 years in prison.

Damn right I'll testify, he snarled. Zat bastard Rivard, he don't bribe nobody.

A movie called The American Trap was made about Rivard's life years later. It dwelt on his alleged involvement with the Kennedy assassination, but it also covered what happened after Frenchy gave him up. He was held for extradition in a Montreal jail, bribed his way out, and was on the lam for four months before being recaptured.

While Rivard was in hiding he wrote letters to various politicians, all copied to the press. In one, addressed to Prime Minister Lester Pearson, he hinted that if he ended up in prison, so would a lot of other people. As a result of the ensuing investigation, Attorney General Guy Favreau resigned. He was replaced by a Quebec MP, Pierre Trudeau, who became Prime Minister of Canada in 1968.

The Canadian Press Association voted Rivard Newsmaker of the Year for 1965, but he was a flash in the pan compared to Frenchy. Wise guys were tripping over each other on their way to the U.S. Attorney's office once Frenchy got the ball rolling. When Rivard's trial in Texas was over the show moved to New England.

Frenchy never let his name slip, but I later found out it was Michel Caron. At first they fed him up in his cell, but after a few days they let him walk across the yard with us for a meal in the mess hall. The guard who escorted him didn't intervene when a big, red-neck truck driver (one of several at Sandstone, all doing time for setting up phony hijackings) bent down nose to nose with Frenchy, called him a snitch and gave him a shove. The one-sided fight that followed ended with Frenchy hoisting his attacker over his head, and body-slamming him on the icy sidewalk. Nobody bothered him after that.

Many well-known informers and men who were otherwise at risk were housed at Sandstone while I was there. Their identities, even their presence, was supposed to be secret, but it was always on the grapevine within days. Joe Valachi, who broke the Mafia code of silence in testimony before Congress, was one of them. There was still a $100,000 price on his head when he died in prison in 1971.

A trustee from Arkansas' Tucker Prison Farm was another. He'd dialed the "Tucker Telephone," an instrument of torture in use there until the early 1960s. We heard he got three years in federal prison when the Justice Department prosecuted some of the Tucker torturers. It was easy to dislike him (I got five for weed, he got three for torture), but I wasn't comfortable condemning Frenchy, or judging someone like Valachi. The snitches I couldn't stomach were the inmates who'd sneak around looking for minor infractions that they could report to the guards. Their only reward was the comfort they derived from kissing the foot that kicked them, but the men they informed on could get weeks in the hole, or even lose good time. Vern turned out to be one of them.

After four weeks in A&O I was assigned to B House, a kind of sorting pen. It was a one-story barracks housing about 150 men, with a day room, a bathroom and four rows of triple-decker bunks. There were aisles between the rows, and stacked footlockers between the bunks. Everybody had a little space, nobody had any privacy.

B House was crowded and noisy by design. The theory was that the occasional psychopath who didn't reveal himself in the relative comfort of A&O would crack under the pressure of B House. Then steps could be taken to isolate or transfer him. A few guys disappeared for that reason while I was in B House, but their presence hardly registered with me.

Most of the men at Sandstone were sentenced out of Chicago, a jurisdiction in which it was unheard of for minor marijuana violators to get the kind of time I did. Therefore, the other inmates thought that there must be more to me than met the casual eye.

It was not a bad reputation to have. Chester Z, one of the "Fanti" (Mafia street soldiers) from Chicago, heard me telling someone that I had no intention of selling the measly amount of marijuana I'd smuggled. He gave me a tip. Tell people here you were dealing, he said. They'll have more respect for you.

It was probably good advice, but I didn't follow it. I was okay with being what I was—a sixties guy, early iteration, kind of a cross between a hipster and a protester. The black inmates liked that, and the white guys were generally not ill-disposed. Paul G, an Italian in his mid-twenties from Rhode Island, was the exception. How come you want to rebel, bring everything down? he'd ask. This is a great country, there's something for everybody here.

Paul couldn't wait to transfer out of B House, but after he was assigned to another barracks he'd seek me out to rag on me about my attitude.

Paul was a gambler, in for fixing college basketball games. "Point shaving," it was called. I couldn't imagine how he went about it. Did he approach a player? A coach? How do you start that conversation? I asked him once, but he just shook his head. He didn't want to talk about that. He wanted to talk about this great country of ours and how long my hair should be. I told him I planned to wear it shoulder-length when I got out just to piss him off.

One day I ran into him in the gym. We shot H-O-R-S-E while he took me to task. He was a slick ball handler, and a dead shot. I was still stuck on O when he sank a 20 footer for E, and about then it dawned on me how he'd shaved points. Chester Z confirmed my theory. Paulie was second team ACC his sophomore year, he said. Could've been a pro.

After a few months I was assigned to A House, where there were fewer inmates and we had cots, not bunks. It was more comfortable, but the time didn't pass any faster. Time was the eternal conundrum. You had to do it, or as the saying goes, it would do you.

We had jobs, which helped fill some time. I was the voucher clerk in the business office. I gathered up supporting documents for each bill the prison received, deducted the standard government discount, and made sure a voucher got to the Cashier (a civil servant, my immediate superior) for a timely payment.

The nature of my work made me privy to certain information everyone wanted, because there were expenditures in connection with those things. For example, I knew ahead of time what the weekly menu would be, a topic of endless fascination. I knew when inmates were being transferred, or when a writ from another jurisdiction came through for someone to appear in court, because I got the bill for transportation. The knowledge gave me a certain low-rent prestige. I tried not to work it, but I got a lot of questions.

There were things I wasn't supposed to know, but I wasn't exactly firewalled. The voucher system was full of holes in that respect, simply because some civil servant in the business office would have to do the work if I didn't. My boss once cautioned me against revealing something that he was supposed to make sure I didn't find out in the first place, the identity of the incompetent old woman who'd been submitting the low bid for anesthesia services since she graduated from nursing school at the dawn of the 20th century. Sometimes a minor procedure that required anesthesia (wiring a broken jaw, removing an impacted molar) was performed at the prison infirmary. She was forever making mistakes that resulted in brain damage or death, and the administration didn't want any friends of the deceased looking her up. I wasn't supposed to be privy to her name, let alone her address, but they were right there on the bills I processed.

Vouchering transportation costs for inmates was a recurring chore, usually when they were released, but occasionally when they had a few days of compassionate leave to attend a funeral or went out on a writ. I also made vouchers for purchases of food, clothing and services of all kinds. I worked eight hours a day, five days a week, just like real people. That left evenings and weekends, which could be interminable. Especially weekends.

Do your own time was the code, meaning don't burden other inmates with your problems. When an inmate, usually young and newly arrived, said that he couldn't do three years, or five years or whatever his sentence was, the standard advice was, "just do what you can."

Tomorrow and tomorrow and tomorrow drags its weary ass from day to day, said Joe Temple, a black guy from St. Paul. Joe should've gone into show business. When he started talking out in the yard a crowd always gathered to hear him. Sometimes he'd be in thespian mode, but usually he did stand-up. It was Joe who told me the crucial difference between junkies and thieves. "They'll both steal your wallet, but the junky will help you look for it."

About half the men in Sandstone, Joe included, were doing five year no-parole sentences. They'd been busted with small amounts of heroin, and prosecuted for "intent to sell," a dubious legal construct in my opinion. Joe and I discussed it once. Surprisingly, he said it was true in some larger sense, though rarely in respect to the circumstances of the actual arrest. We're most of us hope fiends, not dope fiends, he explained. Takes money to be a junky, so we're always hustling—dealin' some, shootin' some. Sooner or later you get set up by a so-called friend who probably got set up by somebody else, and bang! Off to the joint.

Like most heroin offenders, Joe took his sentence in stride, and like most, at least the ones I kept track of, he was dead within a few years of his release. I never heard how he died, just that he was gone. Some died of overdoses, some of liver disease, others were killed as the result of some dumb junky quarrel. Addiction is a life that offers a variety of endings, none of them happy.

Frenchy's comings and goings were one way to measure time. He'd disappear for a week or so then turn up again, a cycle determined by the speed at which the wheel of justice was grinding Lucien Rivard and his gang into dust. Frenchy had been sentenced to ten years, but he freely admitted that he'd be going into witness protection as soon as he finished his end of the deal. You'd think he'd want to get it over with, but as long as Rivard and his people suffered it was time well spent as far as he was concerned. He savored every moment.

Ultimately, Judge Ben C. Connally gave Rivard 20 years. To his regret, Frenchy wasn't there when Rivard was sentenced, but he did get to stick it to him again when the appeal was heard.

One of Rivard's henchmen went to trial in Boston about six months after I entered Sandstone. Frenchy was gone for a couple days, and when he returned he said it might be the last time he had to testify. He was still enjoying it. Zat bastard, he give me the evil eye, but I give him right back. Fock you, I tell him.

The mysterious Caesare V lived in A House. He was older than most of the other inmates, fiftyish, with a swarthy complexion and a five o'clock shadow. He was the next thing to expressionless, mostly silent but when he spoke it was with a thick Italian accent. His prison blues were always clean and pressed, which meant he had someone in the laundry on his payroll. He was said to be a confederate of Sam Giancana's.

Fanti from other barracks would drop by on commissary day and give him candy. Sometimes there'd be a line of them waiting to hand over their little tokens of respect. They were guys who spoke standard Chicago English (we havin' saassich fr'dinner this week?), but when they addressed Caesare they gave his name an old country twist—"Please accept this here gift, Che-sarr-eh." He'd nod, and throw another candy bar in his locker.

Time was marked by events, some out in the world—the Texas Tower killings, the Seven Day War, the Detroit riots—some inside, i.e., The Great Banana Bust.

The English crooner Donovan had a hit called Mellow Yellow in 1966, and somehow the prison authorities got it into their heads that the lyrics meant you could get high on banana peels. They immediately halted sales of bananas in the commissary, and conducted a footlocker search to make sure no one was hoarding any psycho-active fruit on the sly.

A big mound of candy piled up on Caesare's cot when he emptied his locker. The guard sorted through it carefully.

Yes, he found no bananas.

You can put it back now, he said.

Caesare looked him right in the eye. Hows 'bout-a you put it back, he said.

That guard turned gray, and started shoveling candy back in the locker.

One evening Chester Z approached me in the yard and handed me a Milky Way. Caesare wants you to have this, he said. We heard they're turning Frenchy loose tomorrow, and C wants to know where he's headed.

I told him I didn't voucher inmates who were going into witness protection. That was how it was supposed to work. In fact, there had been two men released into witness protection since I was in the business office and I vouchered both of them.

I tried giving the candy bar back, but Chester wouldn't take it. Keep your eyes open just in case, he said. I told him I would.

I wondered if Caesare and his army knew how flawed the security system was. I kept my fingers crossed that it would actually function the way it was supposed to for once, but the next day the bill for Frenchy's air fare was on my desk. It was a direct flight from the Twin Cities to a town in the southeastern U.S. I made the voucher out immediately, and put it on top of the cashier's in-basket, so there was a chance it would get into the mail before anybody else saw it.

Chester came looking for me in the mess hall that evening. Sorry, didn't get the voucher, I told him. Okay, thanks for trying, he said, and gave me another candy bar for my trouble.

Two days later there was a rumor on the grapevine that Frenchy had been shot to death. There were even a few details. He'd been gunned down on the steps of the federal building in New York City, where'd been flown to go into protection. A hit man from Boston got him. Before the day was over everyone knew he was a goner. There was talk about the long arm of the mob, and the many channels of information they cultivated. I tried to read the look on Caesare's face, but he was inscrutable as ever.

Due to a fluke in scheduling I went before the parole board three months before I was eligible for release. Two weeks later, on May 14th, 1967, I found out I'd made parole. My release date was July 31. From then on I was "getting short."

Those 79 days were the hardest time I did. For more than 17 months I'd been stepping on every thought of the outside, but once I knew I'd be leaving that became impossible. I'd lie on my bunk, or space out while I was at work, and run through alternate scenarios for the first day, the first night, the first week.

I must have read 100 books while I was inside, but as my time wound down the only one that could keep me from drifting off into a fantasy of freedom was Huckleberry Finn. I read it three times. I could practically recite old Pap's speech on the island by the time I left.

If I could give some advice to that young man standing in the bus yard in Nuevo Laredo, the one who was about to throw away nearly two years of his life, it would be this: don't be a dope. Nevertheless, as Connor told me back in Laredo, prison wasn't so bad. At worst it was a little depressing, but mostly it was just what it was supposed to be— dull as dog shit, something you'd never repeat if you had an ounce of common sense. I was fortunate to do my time before prisons became warehouses for the mentally ill, and most importantly I wasn't in long enough for it to take a real toll. I heard some good stories, made some friends, a few of them lasting, and made the acquaintance of lots of interesting people I'd never have met otherwise. Some of them became regular sources for me when I started writing true crime stories a decade later, and, of course, I had my own slant on the general topic of crime having committed one and paid the price. That point of view served me well many times in my career as a true crime writer.

The late Judge Ben C. Connally gave me a harsh sentence for a first offender who'd committed a non-violent crime, but it was not off the scale by Texas standards, and Texas was where I chose to transgress, of my own free will. When I judge Judge Connally, which I often did, and still do occasionally, I think of that pronouncement he uttered when he gave Tim Leary 30 years because his daughter inadvertently carried a joint across the border: "You are a menace to the country." Judges are supposed to be judicious, but that sounds kind of hysterical to me. Despite his well-publicized devotion to law and order he was also a central figure in the Laredo marijuana racket, and he gave that scam a pass, so Judge Connally is weighed and found wanting on my scale.

If the experience of imprisonment was supposed to change my behavior it failed. I never was much of a smuggler, and I smoked pot after I got out. Everybody did. I was just more circumspect than most. I haven't smoked for decades, but that's because my respiratory system changed, not my opinion. William Burroughs said it best. Marijuana is a mild tonic with no side effects, a gentle prod to the imagination, nothing more.

I vouchered my own train ticket the day before I left, and didn't sleep at all that night. Next morning I said my good-byes, and spent a few minutes in I&D, on the right side of the ampersand, waiting for a ride to the station. I did not bicker about the ill-fitting pants and ugly shirt they gave me, nor did I fail to say thanks for the toothbrush and the $35 the Federal Bureau of Prisons provided. The guard who took me to town wished me luck.

The train was fifteen minutes late. I paced the platform like a caged animal (except I'd just been sprung from the cage) until

I saw that locomotive coming down the track. Three hours later I disembarked in downtown Minneapolis. I was a little disoriented at first, but pretty soon it was like I'd never been gone.

Acknowledgments

The author wishes to acknowledge the following previous publications. All the necessary permissions have been received:

"The Family That Couldn't Sleep at Night" was serialized in *Sweet Potato*, a Twin Cities Weekly, in 1981. It was re-published in an earlier anthology "Greed Rage and Love Gone Wrong", by the University of Minnesota Press in 2004.

An earlier version of "The Milwaukee Avenue Massacre" was published in *Chicago Magazine* in May 1990, under the title, "Lost in Translation".

"Welcome to Pine County" was published in *City Pages*, a Twin Cities Weekly, in November 1997.

"Danny's Boat" was serialized in *City Pages* in 1986, and re-published in "Greed Rage and Love Gone Wrong".

An earlier version of "Star Stalker" was published in *Chicago Magazine* in February 1992, under the title "The Stalker".

An earlier version of "The Key Man", titled "The Orchid Murder", was published in *Minnesota Journal of Law and*

Politics in 1990, and re-published in "Greed Rage and Love Gone Wrong".

"Last Train" was published in *City Pages* in December 1997, under the title, "Last Train Out".

An earlier version of "The Hanged Priest" was published in *City Pages* in October 2005, under the title, "The Sins of the Fathers".

About the Author

Bruce Rubenstein has published hundreds of true crime stories in weeklies and monthly magazines. In 1991 he received the Chicago Bar Association's Herman Kogan Media Award for his *Chicago Magazine* article about the conviction of four Mexican immigrants for a quadruple homicide (dubbed "The Milwaukee Avenue Massacre" by the *Sun Times*) that they did not commit. They were serving the 9th year of their sentences of life without the possibility of parole when his article came out. As a result of his article the Governor of Illinois pardoned them. An anthology of his crime stories, titled "Greed Rage and Love Gone Wrong", was published by the University Of Minnesota Press in 2004. He won the Minnesota State Arts Council award for fiction in 1979, and published short stories in little magazines in the 70s and 80s. His story, "Smoke got In My eyes", written for the Akashic Books' anthology, Twin Cities Noir (2006), was nominated for the Shamus Award. His fiction has recently appeared in *Ellery Queen's Mystery Magazine*. His book about a notorious art theft titled "The Rockwell Heist" was published by Borealis in March 2013.

www.ingramcontent.com/pod-product-compliance
Lightning Source LLC
Chambersburg PA
CBHW031153270326
41931CB00006B/254